PSYCHOPHYSIOLOGY

PSYCHOPHYSIOLOGY

Some Simple Concepts and Models

By

WALTER W. SURWILLO, Ph.D

Professor
Department of Psychiatry and Behavioral Sciences
University of Louisville School of Medicine
Louisville, Kentucky

CHARLES C THOMAS • PUBLISHER
Springfield • Illinois • U.S.A.

Published and Distributed Throughout the World by
CHARLES C THOMAS • PUBLISHER
2600 South First Street
Springfield, Illinois 62708-4709

© *1986 by* CHARLES C THOMAS • PUBLISHER
ISBN 0-398-05254-9
Library of Congress Catalog Card Number: 86-5780

With **THOMAS BOOKS** *careful attention is given to all details of manufacturing and design. It is the Publisher's desire to present books that are satisfactory as to their physical qualities and artistic possibilities and appropriate for their particular use.* **THOMAS BOOKS** *will be true to those laws of quality that assure a good name and good will.*

Printed in the United States of America
Q-R-3

Library of Congress Cataloging in Publication Data

Surwillo, Walter W.
      Psychophysiology : some simple concepts and models.

      Bibliography: p.
      Includes index.
      1. Psychology, Physiological--Simulation methods.
2. Neuropsychology--Simulation methods. I. Title.
[DNLM: 1. Psychophysiology. WL 103 S963p]
QP360.S87   1986   152   86-5780
ISBN 0-398-05254-9

This book is dedicated to the memory of D. O. Hebb, whose contributions to psychological theory while at McGill University stimulated many of the ideas contained herein.

PREFACE

IN THE *Foundations of Science*, Henri Poincaré wrote the following:

> There is a hierarchy of facts; some have no reach; they teach us nothing but themselves. The scientist who has ascertained them has learned nothing but a fact, and has not become more capable of foreseeing new facts. Such facts, it seems, come once, but are not destined to reappear.
>
> There are, on the other hand, facts of great yield; each of them teaches us a new law. And since a choice must be made, it is to these that the scientist should devote himself.[1]

Today, over 70 years later, it is useful to reflect on these words. With an ever growing and burgeoning body of facts becoming available in all areas of science, it behooves us to follow Poincaré's counsel. Much of present-day knowledge is destined to remain forever in the archives of science—filed away and forgotten. Some of it, on the other hand, will generate new knowledge. But how are we to tell the difference? How can we sort out the facts that are trivial from those that have promise? How can we tell when we are on a potentially fruitful line of inquiry?

In the present writer's belief, it is the richness of the conceptual framework upon which a particular area of science grows and develops that decides these important questions. The history of science has shown this again and again. Without the conceptual insights of Bohr, Einstein and Fermi in the area of nuclear physics, Hahn and Strassmann's demonstration of atomic fission might have been merely an interesting experiment filed away in the archives. In the area of chemistry, Mendeléeff's work on the Periodic Table of the Elements provided a model that brought meaning to a variety of apparently unrelated facts and even predicted the existence of many elements unknown at the time. There are numerous other examples.

---

[1]Poincaré (1913), p. 544.

By its very nature, however, theorizing and the formulation of concepts and models has always been a risky venture for the scientist. For every scientist who takes the risk and says "I think this is how a particular system or process works," a hundred reasons may be found why he or she is wrong. And so, it is often safer just to collect more facts in the hope that new concepts will somehow emerge from them. But science does not work that way. Scientific advances depend upon someone making the venture. It was in this spirit that the present work was undertaken.

Concerning the origin of the concepts with which this volume deals, the writer makes no exclusive claim to their originality. In most cases, I have started with the findings, ideas and insights that originated with others, added a few findings and ideas of my own plus some speculation, and then put it all together in somewhat of a different way. If I have failed to recognize some previous author's priority, I ask the reader to consider the remark of a certain Dr. Brown who, upon being rebuked because he failed to acknowledge some previous work on the subject of his writings, replied: "I made no claim to originality for I have long since found that to consider oneself original one must read nothing at all. All I have done is to describe those methods which I have found to suit me best in practice."[2]

---

[2]Cited by Dawson (1954), p. 65.

ACKNOWLEDGEMENTS

THIS MONOGRAPH was begun during the author's six-month sabbatical at the University, York, England. The courtesy extended to the author by that institution and, in particular, the assistance of Peter Venables, Ph.D. is greatfully acknowledged. The author also wishes to thank John J. Schwab, M.D., Chairman, Department of Psychiatry and Behavioral Sciences at Louisville for his continued support of this work. Finally, a special note of thanks is due to Molly Burke Redett, who typed the entire manuscript and produced many of the illustrations.

CONTENTS

Page

PSYCHOPHYSIOLOGY

CHAPTER 1

THE NATURE OF PSYCHOPHYSIOLOGY

THE PRESENT chapter is a brief picture, in broad outline, of the nature of psychophysiology. It is not intended to be a history of psychophysiology; such a topic would need a volume of its own. Neither does the chapter undertake to review with any philosophical sophistication the age-old, mind-body problem; nor does it discuss fully the implications of the positions taken by monists, dualists, and interactionists in attempting to solve this problem. Such discussions belong, more appropriately, in the realm of the philosophy of science.

So what, then, is the purpose of the present chapter? As the reader will discover, it is merely intended to be a bird's-eye view of what the author thinks current psychophysiology is all about.

Definitions

In general terms, psychophysiology is the scientific study of the relationships between mental and behavioral activities and bodily events. In more specific but limited terms, psychophysiology deals with the interrelationships between *psychological* phenomena which include certain measurable mental, emotional, and motor activities and a variety of *physiological* phenomena that are observable in the intact, behaving organism. Psychophysiology is both similar to and different from physiological psychology which, historically speaking, is considered by some to be the older discipline.[1] Both are concerned with the relationship

---

[1]Some would argue that psychophysiology is the older discipline, citing Helmholtz's attempt in the 19th century to measure nerve conduction velocity in humans using the reaction-time experiment. Others would claim that Hans Berger, the "father" of electroencephalography, was the first real psychophysiologist. Regardless of who or what came first, it seems clear that psychophysiology is a comparatively late bloomer, with progress in the area closely paralleling technological developments in electronics that made polygraphic recording practicable. This is reflected in the chronological history of the periodical literature. Thus, while volume number one of the journal *Psychophysiology* did not come out until 1964, the *Journal of Comparative and Physiological Psychology* first appeared in 1947.

between behavioral activities and bodily events. However, while physiological psychology generally uses animals as subjects, psychophysiology emphasizes the use of human subjects in experimental investigations.

But this is not the major difference between the two areas of investigation. The primary difference seems to be concerned with which of the two phenomena is the *independent* and which the *dependent* variable in an experiment. In a typical experiment reported by a physiological psychologist, the independent variable is the physiological phenomenon while the dependent variable is behavior. In most psychophysiological studies, on the other hand, the experimental design is reversed. Behavior is the variable that the investigator manipulates in some way, while one or more physiological phenomena serve as the dependent variable (Stern, 1964). Two different, major points of view are encountered in such experiments. Some psychophysiologists treat the physiological events as *determinants* of behavior while others consider them to be simply aspects or *concomitants* of behavior.

Either viewpoint implies the existence of a model that defines the overall relationship between the physiological and psychological phenomena involved. The model in one case is quite different from the model in the other. Both models, however, are definitional — and primitive in the sense of defining certain rudimentary principles. Each incorporates the essential essence of a different philosophy of science.

Primitive Definitional Models

The viewpoint which treats physiological events as *determinants* of behavior assumes the existence of a *series* model in which psychological phenomena are thought to be preceded and determined by physiological events. As shown in Figure 1a, physiological events are elicited by the organism and these, in turn, lead to psychological events. The later include different varieties of behavior which, it is presumed, are uniquely defined by some specific physiological events. The series model, therefore, is causally based in that a particular behavior cannot take place except in the presence of the appropriate physiological events. This model breaks down whenever a divergence is observed between the physiological and psychological phenomena involved.

In assuming that physiological events are *concomitants* of behavior, a *parallel* model is inferred in which physiological and psychological phenomena are treated as two different aspects of the same process. No mystical mind-body relationship is implied as both phenomena are considered to take place concurrently in the same biological organism. Each is viewed as a phenomenon in its own right; and, as seen in Figure 1b, primacy is given to neither. Psychological events may be predicted from physiological events or *vice versa,* but no causal relationship is assumed or implied between them. This contrasts sharply with the series model in which physiological events are considered to be the precursors of psychological events. Because neither phenomenon is considered to be essential to the other, the parallel model does not break down whenever there is a divergence or lack of correspondence between physiological and psychological processes that take place concurrently.

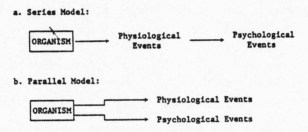

Figure 1: Primitive models defining the relationship between physiological and psychological events. Psychological Events are behaviors that include mental and emotional states and activities, as well as voluntary motor activities.

Goals and Objectives

The overall goal of psychophysiology is to discover the laws which unite psychological and physiological phenomena. In actual practice, however, the objectives have been much more limited. Four such limited but major objectives can be identified.

One major objective of psychophysiology is to find out in what way various observable physiological events or phenomena are related to stimulation of the various sensory channels and to performance on a variety of perceptual and cognitive tasks. Inherent in this goal is the need for an adequate methodology—for techniques of measuring physiological phenomena that are accurate, reliable, and valid. A second objective is to determine the range of variation of a variety of measurable physiological phenomena so as to define the limits of normal physiological functioning. While the emphasis here is on gathering normative data, the ultimate goal is to discover whether normal variations in particular physiological functions are associated with shifts in certain behavioral states or with variations in the way certain tasks and activities are carried out. Additionally, the presence of various pathological changes in both behavior and physiological functioning leads naturally to a consideration of the psychosomatic disorders.

A third objective of psychophysiology is to discover whether some important psychological phenomena have physiological correlates that are accessible to measurement. Among the phenomena that have attracted considerable interest are aspects of behavior such as attention, emotion, and motivation. Finally, the fourth major objective of psychophysiology is to develop some plausible concepts and models whereby knowledge of physiological states and events may be used to clarify psychological concepts and to explain some aspects of psychological functioning. Where the series type of definitional model is adopted, such model building is concerned with identifying some of the *physiological mechanisms* of behavior.

Psychophysiology as the Search for Physiological Referents — Ax's Computer Analogy

Ax (1964) has suggested that the primary goal of psychophysiology is the discovery of the physiological "referents" for the concepts used in psychology. This goal has been defined and discussed in a unique way by the use of an interesting analogy involving computers.[2] Computers, Ax reminds us, may be described in different ways. An engineer describes a computer in terms of its actual circuits using the machine language as a vehicle of expression. The computer programmer does the same thing but by means of a symbolic programming system without any reference to the circuit hardware. Figure 2 diagrams these relationships.

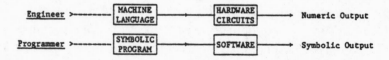

Figure 2: Two ways of describing computer systems.

---

[2]The analogy between the brain and the computer, of course, was not new with Ax. Norbert Wiener's landmark treatise entitled *Cybernetics,* that appeared in 1948, contained a chapter on computing machines and the nervous system. Prior to that time, McCulloch and Pitts (1943) were investigating the architecture of nervous activity using the technique of mathematical logic — a method that was applied later to the design of computing machines.

In his computer analogy, Ax likens soma or the brain to the machine language and hardware of a computer while psyche is analogous to the symbolic program and software. Physiology, on the one hand, describes the soma in the same way that an engineer describes a computer whereas psychology, on the other, describes the psyche much like a programmer describes the symbolic program. In the domain of computers, a specific set of rules exists whereby a symbolic program and the machine language are related. These rules are embodied in the *translator* or specific translator program that converts every command of the symbolic program into the computer's own machine language.

To complete the analogy, Ax believes that a similar set of rules exists in the case of biological organisms. It is by means of these rules that the two domains of physiology and psychology interact and are related. Psychophysiology, he states, is concerned with the interface between these two disciplines. Correspondingly, the psychophysiologist's objective is to study the *organismic translator* and to discover the rules whereby psychological processes become translated into physiological functioning which, in turn, is translated into behavior. Figure 3 details these relationships, both in the case of computers and biological systems. It will be seen that behavior comes out of the biological organism in the same way that the computational output is generated by the computer hardware. This is not to say, of course, that computers and men are alike; only the plans upon which the two systems function appear to show interesting similarities.

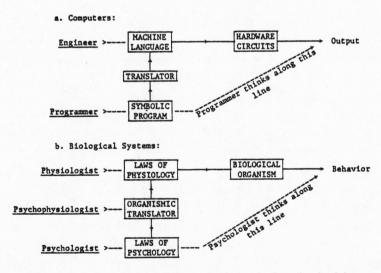

Figure 3: Ax's computer analogy and the goal of psychophysiology.

Realization of Objectives

Where do we presently stand with regard to the major objectives of psychophysiology? Concerning the first objective, considerable effort has been devoted to investigating the physiological events associated with sensory stimulation and with performance on various perceptual and cognitive tasks. A wealth of such data is found in the literature. For example, we know a great deal about how the galvanic skin reflex changes in relation to changes in the parameters of stimulation. How average evoked cortical potentials vary with differences in the character and meaning of a stimulus and with the properties of a response has been exhaustively investigated. Changes in pulse rate in relation to a wide variety of stimulus conditions have been minutely detailed. Indeed, the way in which nearly every accessible physiological phenomenon varies in relation to a wide range of stimulus conditions and to performance on a variety of tasks—from simple responding to complex cognitive activities—has been studied.

In regard to the second major objective, there are numerous normative studies of physiological phenomena such as the electroencephalogram (EEG), pulse rate, and the electrical resistance of the skin. These phenomena have been investigated in relation to variables such as age and different behavioral states. Besides helping to define the normal range of human conciousness, such studies have contributed to our understanding of phenomena like sleep and dreaming. But the greater share of psychophysiological research has been devoted to the pursuit of the third major objective. Investigations of aspects of behavior such as attention, emotion and motivation or of what is often termed "arousal" have accounted for a sizable portion of the psychophysiological literature.

When we come to the fourth major objective of psychophysiology, the picture of progress changes dramatically. It is noteworthy that, upon assuming the editorship of the journal *Psychophysiology,* David Shapiro (1978) wrote that "Theoretical papers dealing with conceptual problems in the field are sorely needed . . . the long standing problem of psychophysiology is the lack of any coherent conceptual framework for our joint interests . . ." Even today, comparatively little space in the psychophysiological literature is devoted to the development of concepts and models. Moreover, efforts to discover the physiological referents of concepts used in psychology, and attempts to delineate the physiological mechanisms of behavior, have not met with notable success. Two factors are considered by some to be responsible. Some persons claim that psychophysiology is still in its infancy and for this reason sufficient hard data are not available to permit systematic model building. Others argue that we presently lack adequate methodology for discovering the relationships that would facilitate the development of useful concepts and powerful models. One example of this way of thinking is the belief that the significance of the spontaneous electrical activity of the brain will remain obscure until some new, hitherto unknown method of analyzing the EEG is discovered.

The critical importance of such factors in the development of concepts and models in science can hardly be denied. No science can flourish in the absence of a sufficient body of facts. Nor can the necessary facts become available without the methodology requisite to successful experimentation. But who is to say when sufficient factual information is at hand for fruitful concepts development and useful model building? It is the present writer's belief that, regardless of how limited or imperfect it may be, some kind of conceptual framework is essential both for organizing existing knowledge and for generating new information. The present work is an attempt at a systematic effort in that direction.

CHAPTER 2

PRESENT-DAY CONCEPTS IN PSYCHOPHYSIOLOGY

BEFORE GOING INTO the material for which this work was intended, it will be useful to take a brief look at the current status of conceptual thinking in psychophysiology. Our purpose is not to provide an extensive critique of the area. Rather, the intention is to present, in broad picture, some of the major concepts that have commanded the attention of psychophysiologists in recent years.

Character of Present-Day Concepts

That psychophysiology does not possess a vigorous program of conceptual thinking is readily apparent from an examination of any undergraduate textbook in the area. Consider, for example, Andreassi's (1980) recent textbook entitled, *Psychophysiology: Human Behavior and Physiological Response*. In a short chapter devoted to concepts in psychophysiology, Andreassi remarks rather apologetically that psychophysiology does not have an all-inclusive conceptual framework. Instead, he says, it has a number of concepts, some old and some new. Andreassi observes that some of the concepts contradict one another. He then goes on to enumerate and briefly discuss a total of eight concepts. These concepts are the law of initial value, autonomic balance, activation or "arousal," stimulus response specificity, individual response specificity, cardiac-somatic coupling, adaptation and rebound, and orienting and defensive reactions.

The eight concepts listed by Andreassi are heavily slanted towards autonomic nervous system psychophysiology; thus, with the exception of activation, all of them deal almost exclusively with the functioning of the autonomic nervous system. They are chiefly the offspring of a viewpoint that sees psychophysiology mainly as the science of taking and interpreting polygraphic recordings. It will be instructive to examine a few of these concepts in more detail and get the flavor of present-day conceptual thinking.

The Law of Initial Value

The Law of Initial Value, or LIV, is a concept that deals with the magnitude and direction of physiological responses in relation to the initial or prestimulus level of the physiological system under investigation. The law states that, the higher the initial level of a physiological function, the smaller will be the response to stimuli that produce an increment and the larger the response to stimuli that produce a decrement. Furthermore, when the intitial level is an extreme value, there is a tendency for no apparent response or even a "paradoxical" response to occur to stimulation. Paradoxical responses are those which are in the reverse of the expected direction. The LIV, which was first formulated by Wilder in 1930, originated in a study of the autonomic nervous system (see Wilder, 1967). Wilder introduced the concept as a means of bringing some harmony into the apparent inconsistencies observed in the reactions of different individuals to atropine, adrenaline, and pilocarpine. Although the original research dealt only with changes in pulse rate and systolic blood pressure, Wilder considered the LIV to apply to all responses that are under the control of the autonomic nervous system.

Predictions based on the LIV are frequently not substantiated in psychophysiological research. Indeed the law does not seem to hold at all pre-stimulus levels, for all subjects, or for all psychophysiological measures. This has led Stern, Ray, and Davis (1980) to observe in their textbook that the concept would be better formulated as a "principle" than as a law.

A careful perusal of the LIV reveals that the law, in reality, is a model for measuring change and should be applicable to the measurement of any kind of variable. Other ways of stating the law is to say that a "ceiling effect" operates to limit extreme values of a variable, or that whatever goes up must come down and vice versa. In other words, there is a ubiquitous tendency in natural phenomena for the magnitude of a change to be in proportion to the level from which this change occurs. But this is similar to a phenomenon that has been termed the "regression effect" in the measurement literature (see e.g., Lord, 1963). According to the regression effect, measures at the extremes of a distribution will, when they are replicated, show a tendency to be less extreme, or to "regress" in the direction of the mean of the distribution. Thus, for example, if two measurements of any variable are made on each individual in a group, and a straight line is fitted to a graph of these data, the slope of the regression line — measurement 2 being the Y variable and measurement 1 the X variable — will be less than unity.

How do we know in a particular case whether the LIV is any different from the regression effect? This is a question that can be answered empirically by controlling for the regression effect. It has been suggested that a control group be added in all investigations of the LIV to assess the magnitude of the regression effect (Surwillo and Arenberg, 1965). Unfortunately, however, this line of investigation has not been pursued so that the question still remains unanswered (e.g., see Scher, Furedy and Heslegrave, 1985).

Autonomic Balance

Autonomic balance is a concept that deals with the extent to which the sympathetic nervous system or parasympathetic nervous system is dominant in an individual. The concept derives from the earlier concepts of vagotonia and sympathicotonia that were first formulated by Eppinger and Hess (1915).[1] As was true in the case of the law of initial value, vagotonia and sympathicotonia were proposed as a way of explaining differences in the responses of various individuals to certain drugs. According to this terminology, persons who showed vigorous response to stimulation of the sympathetic nervous system but sluggish response to parasympathetic stimulation were sympathicotonic. Persons who showed the opposite, namely, slight response to stimulation of the sympathetic but excessive response to stimulation of the parasympathetic nervous system were called vagotonic.

Wenger and his associates (Wenger, 1941, 1948, 1966; Wenger and Cullen, 1972; Wenger and Ellington, 1943) modified and extended Eppinger and Hess' notions by developing a way of quantifying the phenomenon. The degree to which either the sympathetic or parasympathetic nervous system is dominant in an individual was estimated by an empirically-determined, weighted score designated $\overline{A}$ or autonomic balance. A person's $\overline{A}$ was a composite score, statistically derived from a number of autonomically controlled variables that were recorded under resting conditions in the group of individuals to which this person belonged. These variables included measures of palmar and forearm skin conductance, respiration rate, heart period, pulse pressure, salivation, and red dermographia. Wenger found that the distributions of $\overline{A}$ scores in groups of children and adults were approximately normal.

---

[1] Actually, efforts to categorize individuals according to dominant tendencies in their makeup can be traced back to the four personality types identified by the Greeks.

The concept of autonomic balance as embodied in the $\overline{A}$ score, is a statistical one. It describes the apparent relative dominance of sympathetic and parasympathetic activity only with reference to the other individuals in the group on whom $\overline{A}$ scores were obtained. Thus, high $\overline{A}$ scores are indicative of parasympathetic nervous system dominance while low $\overline{A}$ scores reflect sympathetic nervous system dominance *relative* to the scores of the other individuals in the group. Standardization on a group taken from the population at large appears not to have been carried out. This may account for the fact that few studies have been performed to test and expand this concept.

Activation or "Arousal"

This has been a very popular concept for over 30 years. Its popularity derives from its apparent simplicity and wide applicability. The concept of activation attempts to explain changes that occur in behavior in terms of variations in level of physiological activity. Behavior is thought to have two different dimensions or major characteristics, namely, the goal toward which the behavior is directed at a particular instant, and the intensity with which it is carried out. The latter characteristic, the intensity of behavior, is termed activation or arousal and is thought to be reflected in the level of responsiveness in a number of physiological variables. Increasing levels of pulse rate, blood pressure, tonic muscle tension, and skin conductance, for example, are related to increased activation, while decreased levels of these same variables would indicate lowered activation. Similarly, the presence of fast activity (beta) in the electroencephalogram is indicative of high levels of activation, while slower activity (alpha and theta) indicates lower levels of activation.

The concept of activation has been formulated and used by a number of investigators; chief among them have been Duffy (1962), Hebb (1955), Lindsley (1951), and Malmo (1959). The primary tenent of the concept is that level of performance rises with increases in physiological activity up to a point that is optimal for a particular task; beyond this point, further increases in activation cause a drop in performance. Thus, the basic proposition of this concept is that performance on any task is optimal at some intermediate level of activation. This means that the relationship between performance and activation is described by an inverted-U shaped curve. By way of example, performance on a task would be poor when a person is drowsy and activation is very low. As the person becomes more alert, performance improves until it reaches an optimum with moderate levels of activation. But as activation increases further so that the person becomes very excited and panicky, performance would deteriorate.

Andreassi (1980) has reviewed the empirical evidence which both supports and refutes this interesting concept. The concept has proven to be a very robust one. Thus, studies that have failed to support the concept are easily disposed of on the grounds that the activation levels dealt with were either insufficiently high or insufficiently low to display the inverted-U relationship. A weakness of the concept pointed out by Andreassi is its lack of precision in specifying an optimal physiological level for the individuals performing a particular task. It is easy to assume that individuals whose performance on a task is positively correlated with activation level are functioning on the left side of the optimal point on the inverted-U curve, while those whose performance is negatively correlated with activation level are functioning on the right side. The hazard of making such assumptions — namely, the artificial generation of an inverted-U function when data from the different individuals are combined — has already been pointed out (Surwillo, 1965, 1967).

One problem with the concept is the fact that the different physiological variables proposed as indices of activation are themselves only poorly correlated. How can all the variables be measuring the same thing if they have little if any variance in common? This problem has been difficult to resolve. Aside from postulating that there are different varieties of arousal — cortical, autonomic, cardiac as opposed to respiratory, etc. — there is no real solution. But doing so destroys the apparent generality of the concept which has mainly been responsible for its appeal. Despite these problems, however, arousal has been and continues to be a central concept in psychophysiology. For nearly a generation, it has provided psychologists with concrete evidence that psychophysiology is alive and exists as a discipline in its own right.

Stimulus Response Specificity

Stimulus response specificity deals with the pattern of activity that occurs in various physiological functions. According to this concept, the pattern of physiological response in any individual depends upon the stimulus situation. Thus, for example, if a particular stimulus situation produces a response consisting of an increase in one physiological function but a decrease in another, a different stimulus situation may result in both of those functions changing in the same direction. In other words, different patterns of physiological response go along with different patterns of stimulation. Ax (1953) tested the validity of this concept when he investigated the question of whether fear and anger could be distinguished by differences in the pattern of physiological response to these emotions.

Lacey (1959, 1967) developed and greatly expanded the scope of this concept. Lacey's interest was focused on the divergent patterns that occurred in the pulse rate and skin conductance responses to different stimulus situations. Although skin conductance regularly showed increases during performance on a variety of behavioral tasks, pulse rate increased during performance on some tasks but decreased during performance on others. Lacey (1959) referred to this phenomenon as the "directional fractionation of response," and presented evidence which showed that tasks involving cognitive functioning—e.g., thinking—are accompanied by increases in pulse rate while those emphasizing perceptual activity, as, for example, visual attention, lead to pulse rate deceleration. These findings suggested a novel hypothesis, namely, that cardiac deceleration facilitates "intake" of environmental stimuli, while cardiac acceleration is associated with attempts to exclude or "reject" stimuli that would be disruptive to cognitive functioning.

In later work (Lacey, 1967) the "intake-rejection" hypothesis was refined and a mechanism was proposed whereby cardiac deceleration plays an important role in the regulation of brain functioning. According to this model, changes in pulse rate and blood pressure can influence cortical activity thereby affecting sensitivity to stimulation. The change is mediated via the baroreceptors in the carotid and aortic arteries. A decrease in the pulse rate and blood pressure results in decreased afferent feedback from the baroreceptors to cortical areas, thereby causing increased cortical activity. Elevated cardiovascular activity, on the other hand, increases baroreceptor feedback and inhibits cortical activity. These propositions are inferences based primarily on evidence from animal studies which show that cardiovascular activity can affect frequency of the EEG, with decreased baroreceptor feedback being associated with increased EEG frequency and increased baroreceptor feedback associated with EEG slowing.

Conceptual Thinking and Event-Related Brain Potentials

An area that is beginning to show some promise in conceptual thinking and model building is that concerned with evoked brain electrical activity. Computer methods of coherent averaging have made it possible to record quite readily the brain's minutest responses to various different stimuli in a wide variety of stimulus situations. These methods have revealed that evoked brain electrical activity can tell us a great deal about the psychological phenomena that take place with stimulation and the arrival of its effects at the level of the cerebral cortex. A case in point is one of the long-latency components of event-related potentials. This component, which is designated as P3 or the third major positive component following stimulation, has been implicated in cognitive activity.

A number of different concepts and models have developed around the P3 component. Donchin (1981) has conceived of P3 as underlying or representing the physiological processes whereby schemas devised by the brain are revised so that the context in which a stimulus is interpreted by the observer is continually updated. Callaway (1983) used P3 in a serial information processing model devised to study the effects of age and drugs on human information processing. In his model, P3 is the key element, and the parameters of P3 are related conceptually to the process of stimulus evaluation. Yet more recently, Grossberg (1984) used P3 as the major physiological event in a mathematically-based developmental, cognitive, and motivational theory of behavior.

Appraisal

As was mentioned at the beginning of this chapter, concepts in psychophysiology show a strong preference for phenomena associated with the autonomic nervous system. Those springing from recent work in the area of event-related brain potentials are notable exceptions. Of the sample of four concepts that we have examined in detail, three are concerned primarily with explaining some aspect of autonomic functioning.

In the main, the concepts themselves are very general, broad statements. Thus, for example, autonomic balance encompasses the functioning of the entire autonomic nervous system. Or, to cite another example, activation is thought to be one of the two primary dimensions of behavior. The same can be said of all the concepts listed at the beginning of this chapter. Even the recent theorizing in the area of event-related potentials encompasses broad, general concepts—e.g., context updating and schema revision.

The generality that is characteristic of the concepts in psychophysiology is both a strength and a weakness. The strength lies in the presumed applicability of the concepts to a wide range of human behavior. But by attempting to cover a wide area, their depth is severely restricted. If it turned out, for example, that 5 out of 6 physiological functions did in fact vary with performance on a wide variety of different tasks according to an inverted-U shaped curve, what would this relationship tell us about how the structure and function of the nervous system account for the behavior? What brain mechanisms would this relationship make explicit? In other words, like facts that teach us nothing but themselves, the theoretical reach of such global concepts is limited.

What direction, then, should conceptual development and model building in psychophysiology take? Of one fact we are certain. Unless some new and unique discovery is forthcoming, human behavior must somehow emerge from the simple units — the neurons and synapses — of which the nervous system is composed. For this reason, it seems necessary that concepts in psychophysiology address the questions of how such units are organized and what mechanisms are involved in behavior. Hebb expressed this simply and succinctly when he stated that "The problem of understanding behavior is the problem of understanding the total action of the nervous system and vice versa.[2] With this proposition as a starting point, let us see how far we can go.

---

[2]Hebb (1949), p. xiv.

CHAPTER 3

CONCEPTUAL SIMPLICITY AND THE STRATEGY OF MODEL BUILDING

IN LAUNCHING an undertaking such as this, some general guide-lines are necessary. Human behavior can assume a myriad variety of forms. What kinds of behavior should we endeavor to model?

Simplicity vs. Complexity

Much of theory and model building in human psychology has been concerned with behavior and phenomena that are quite complex. This is hardly surprising considering the nature of psychology. Topics of interest to most psychologists — as, for example, learning, memory, the thought process, and motivation — are incredibly complex. There are, of course, exceptions to this and some of them have experienced significant growth and development in the realm of concepts. Research dealing with the orientating response (Lynn, 1966; Sokolov, 1963a), conditioning (Sokolov, 1963b), and choice reaction time (Luce and Green, 1972; Smith, 1980) are notable examples. But by and large, complex phenomena and intelligent behavior are what have captured the interest of the vast majority of psychologists.

For the most part, the same seems to be true of psychophysiology. Psychophysiological research also has shown a preference for the more complex behavioral phenomena. The history of EEG research is a case in point. During the 1930's and 40's, interest focussed on investigations of the EEG correlates of complex mental processes. There was a belief that EEG based research would help to unravel the mysteries of the thought processes. But these ambitious hopes faded; for despite the fact that the EEG was found to be correlated with numerous mental events, the correlations all proved to be disappointingly low. Subsequently, interest turned to the EEG as a possible physiological index of activation or "arousal." Again, however, the results failed to come up to original expectations; the EEG proved not to be a simple yardstick of arousal.

In the belief that there is merit in trying to understand simple behavior first before attempting to explain the more complex behaviors of which humans are capable, the present work proposes to deal only with the simplest kinds of behavior. The goal is to devise a physiologically-based conceptual framework that is plausible, and to construct a model that is capable of eliciting some of the more important features of simple behavior.

Simple Behavior and Simple Concepts

What is simple behavior? What are the simplest activities that a human being is capable of carrying out? Clearly, the various reflexes and the orientating response would qualify as being the simplest; but these are involuntary activities. If we specify a voluntary act, a little thought will show that the simplest activity possible is the performance of a reaction task—as when a subject takes part in a reaction-time (RT) experiment.

At first glance, the RT experiment hardly seems to be of any great psychological or psychophysiological interest. A stimulus is presented and the subject recognizes that the stimulus requires a response. He or she responds, and the latency of the response—the RT—is accurately measured. But a close look at what is presently known about the RT reveals that little is understood about what happens during this brief interval. Why, for example, should some individuals respond more quickly than others? Or why should RT vary from one trial to the next in the same individual? To say that these differences are explained by variations in arousal or attention simply begs the question and has the flavor of tautology.

The plain fact is that we do not know what is responsible for RT variability either within or between individuals. This is one aspect of the phenomenon that makes it of interest psychophysiologically. Another concerns the fact that the RT becomes longer as the amount of information transmitted by the stimulus increases. Thus, it is common knowledge that disjunctive RT—or a reaction involving some choice or decision—is longer than simple RT. But the precise way in which the additional time is consumed is unknown.

What are the distinguishing features of simple concepts? In what ways do they differ from complex concepts? To be of psychophysiological relevance, what characteristics must a concept display? In the first place, simple concepts are invariably unitary. They are clearly defined along a single dimension as opposed to complex concepts which are frequently multidimensional. Simple concepts are concerned with the essence of a phenomenon whereas complex concepts frequently deal with details or minor aspects of it. Finally, to be of psychophysiological relevance, concepts need to be firmly based physiologically.

Elements in a Model of Simple Behavior

A minimum of three elements is necessary. These are a sensing element or receptor, a responding element or effector, and a connecting element that serves as an information transmission system between receptor and effector. For present purposes, the information transmission system is the element that will interest us the most.

Present-day knowledge of neurophysiology tells us a great deal about the information transmission system. This knowledge is embodied in a few simple facts. Assuming that neuroglial tissue is not involved in the transmission of information, the basic unit or building block of this system is the neuron. As more than one neuron may be involved, the information transmission system is frequently a multi-unit element. In the human nervous system, information travels from one contiguous neuron to another, there being no evidence that ephatic conduction plays any part in the process. It can be concluded, therefore, that the parameters of transmission will be determined by (1) the characteristics of the neuron or neurons in the chain between receptor and effector and (2) the characteristics of the junctions between receptor and neuron, neuron and neuron if there is more than one in the chain, and neuron and effector.

The junction or interface between any of the elements is commonly referred to as the synapse. Transmission in the neuron is an electrical event while conduction across the synapse is chemical. The neuron is an all-or-none device, with the intensity of stimulation coded in terms of the frequency of neuronal discharge. In other words, the neuron has two distinct stable states, these states being either firing or resting. The all-or-none character of a neuron's discharge is precisely analogous to the single choice made in determining a digit on the binary scale. It is interesting to note that, long before the advent of modern digital computers, Wiener (1948) pointed out that a device like the neuron would be the most satisfactory building block upon which to base the design of computing machines.

The simplest configuration of these elements consists of a receptor (R) and an effector (E) with a single neuron between. This is shown in Figure 4 in which the gaps between the elements are synapses. The purpose of the neuron is readily apparent from a perusal of the diagram. If R were connected directly to E, the system would have no flexibility, with E always being at the mercy of R. In other words, E would be activated whenever R was stimulated and E's threshold was exceeded.

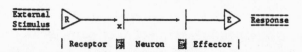

Figure 4: Simplest configuration of elements in a model of simple behavior. Shaded areas represent the junctions or synapses between the elements.

The intervening neuron allows the response of the effector to be modulated. The result can be achieved in two different ways, either (1) by the occurrence of variations in the excitability of the neuron, or (2) by the introduction of another neuron at point "x" in Figure 4. This is shown in Figure 5 where the original neuron is designated "*a*" and the additional neuron is designated "*b*." Note that neuron *b* and R both impinge on the same synapse. By suitable adjustment of its threshold, neuron *a* may only be activated whenever both of these elements are activated simultaneously, and the summation of the two effects exceeds neuron *a*'s threshold. In this context, the synapse is simply a mechanism for determining whether a certain combination of outputs from some impinging elements will or will not act as an adequate stimulus for the discharge of the next element. Neuron *b*, which we refer to as the "gating" neuron, represents a fourth element in our model of simple behavior. It is essential in that, together with neuron *a*, it provides an external means of modulating effector response without changing effector sensitivity. As we shall see later, the "gating" neuron also provides a way of synchronizing E's response with all other effector activities within the organism.

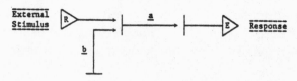

Figure 5: Model of simple behavior shown in Figure 4 with the addition of neuron *b*, the "gating" neuron.

The simple system diagramed in Figure 5 affords no flexibility as far as R is concerned. It is clearly apparent from this figure that the only effect of R being active is the elicitation of a response from E. This situation can be remedied by providing a stage of parallel neurons, c_1, c_2, . . . c_n, between R and neuron a as shown in Figure 6. These parallel neurons serve to distribute the effects of stimulating R to other effectors within the whole organism. Note that neuron c_1 is connected to neuron a and thence to E. The other c neurons are free to be hooked up in the same way to other effectors.

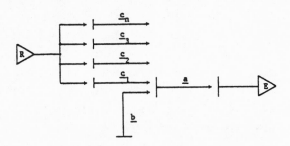

Figure 6: Model shown in Figure 5 with the addition of parallel interconnecting neurons c_1, c_2, . . . c_n.

The Gating Neuron and the Concept of Timing

In the simple model shown in Figure 5, an effector response will be produced whenever (1) a stimulus impinges on R, and (2) the gating neuron b is simultaneously activated and (3) the threshold of neuron a is exceeded. The same will be true of the model in Figure 6 except that the impulse arriving from the receptor will be delayed by the time consumed at an additional synapse and by the conduction time of neuron c. The timing relations (ignoring recovery time of the neurons) of these events are diagramed in Figure 7. It is assumed that the gating neuron is activated periodically so that gating signals occur regularly in time. Note that the gating neuron permits the response to take place only at a certain time, i.e., when a gating signal is present and neuron c is active.

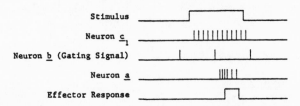

Figure 7: Timing diagram for the circuit shown in Figure 6.

By making the effector response dependent upon the presence of a gating signal as well as the stimulus, the latency of response on the average will be longer and more variable. This results from the fact that, whenever the start of a stimulus fails to occur in close proximity to a gating signal, the response is delayed until the next gating signal comes along. But in sacrificing speed, some flexibility is gained. Thus, a response can be avoided whenever a gating signal is absent — even though an otherwise adequate stimulus has occurred. In this way, a measure of control over the effects of stimulation is achieved.

But there is a far more important reason for having a gating signal than to modulate the response of the single receptor-effector system. At any one time, numerous systems like the one shown in Figure 6 can be functioning within the body of a complex organism. Without the control of the gating neurons, the timing of the effector responses in all these systems would be determined solely by the excitability of the neurons involved and would be wholly under the control of the various stimuli bombarding the organism. This would present a chaotic situation indeed, with muscles contracting here and there without any overall temporal organization to the activities. By limiting effector responses so they occur only at specific times as determined by a periodically-occurring gating signal, a smooth and orderly coordination of these activities can be achieved. In this way, the various individual receptor-effector systems which form the building blocks of behavior can function in concert.

The gating neuron may be thought of as the local manifestation of a central timing device. The need for such a device in the brain is analogous to the need for a conductor in an orchestra. Indeed, the central timing device has a function similar to that of the conductor. Just as the various instrumentalists take their beat from the conductor, so in the present model do the various receptor-effector systems in the organism function according to the rhythm of the central timing device. The periodic gating signals of the central timing device suggest similarities to the cycle time in computers. If such a similarity does indeed exist, the interval between consecutively-occurring gating signals would correspond to the time quantum of the system — the minimum time necessary for the system to process a single unit of information. But more about this in a later chapter.

Alternatives to Central Timing

Our contention that central timing is an essential concept for a model of behavior may be critically appraised by considering the alternatives to central timing. In what other ways may activities initiated by the different sense modalities, or activities carried out by different effectors or by effectors on both sides of the body be coordinated in time? In other words, how otherwise than through some central timing mechanism can two or more separate systems like that shown in Figure 4 be made to work in coordination with or in harmony with each other, assuming that the overall system of which they are a part functions according to principles similar to those that govern the functioning of a digital computing machine?

It is easy to see that there are two major possibilities. In order for the systems to be coordinated in time, all of them would need either to be functionally alike in the time domain so that stimulation of either would elicit a pre-programmed response simultaneously at both effectors, or else one of the receptor-effector systems would need to exert some kind of control over the others. The former possibility is what we find in a so-called hard-wired or pre-wired system. Such systems are inflexible and can perform only the limited functions for which they were designed. This being the case, every variety of behavior that an organism was capable of performing would need to have a separate, pre-wired system to produce it. Evidently, this is what we have in purely reflex behavior, and it may be the case in some forms of instinctive behavior. But there is no evidence that the human brain is organized in such a way that a separate circuit is set aside for each different behavior of which the organism is capable of producing.

The idea of one receptor-effector system exerting control over all the others concerned in a particular behavioral sequence is an attractive alternative to central timing as a means of coordinating left- and right-sided activities. This type of control is implicit in the concept of cerebral dominance, and the existence of the corpus callosum provides the anatomic basis whereby a receptor-effector system on one side could exert control over receptor-effector systems on the other. If this control extended to coordination in the time domain, we should expect behavior requiring coordination in time of effectors on both sides of the body to be severely impaired in persons whose corpus callosums were sectioned. But this does not appear to be the case.

Physiological Basis of Central Timing

If the idea of central timing were indeed a reality, what periodic physiologic function could serve as the timing mechanism? An obvious candidate is the spontaneous, rhythmic electrical activity of the brain—the electroencephalogram or EEG. As a matter of fact, the notion that rhythmic brain electrical activity might be implicated in the regulation of brain function has been a recurrent theme since the 1930's. The idea appears to have originated with Bishop's (1933, 1936) speculation that the alpha rhythm of the EEG is associated with a cortical excitability cycle. This was followed by (1) Lindsley's (1952) proposal that alpha activity provides a means of pulsing and coding sensory impulses, (2) Walter's (1950, 1953) suggestion that the alpha rhythm is a scanning function that serves as a central regulating mechanism for coordinating afferent and efferent signals, (3) Wiener's (1958) hypothesis that the alpha rhythm serves the function of a "clock" in the organization of behavior, and (4) Gooddy's (1958) notion that the brain is a clock and the alpha rhythm of the EEG the beat according to which it functions.

The idea of identifying the spontaneous, rhythmic electrical activity of the brain with the temporal organization of behavior has not, in recent years, received much attention. This is unfortunate, as the concept of central timing appears to be so essential and there is, at present, no other known periodic brain phenomenon that could serve as a physiological basis for central timing. For these reasons, the writer has elected to accept as a working hypothesis that the alpha rhythm or posterior-dominant rhythm of the brain is the physiological basis of central timing. We will see where this hypothesis leads us with our model, and then evaluate the model in the light of available evidence.

Origin of the EEG

There is an extensive literature available concerning the origin of the spontaneous electrical activity of the brain. A thorough review and assessment of this material would require a volume of its own. For purposes of the present work, the research of Andersen and Andersson (1968) concerning origin provides the basis for our model. Briefly, Andersen and Andersson conceive the EEG as originating in a group of pacemaker neurons that are located in the thalamus and project diffusely to the cerebral cortex. It has been reported that these units can spread their effects over a wide area of the cortex. The pacemaker neurons are believed to be capable of synchronizing the activity in large numbers of cortical neurons. By Elul's (1972) estimate, synchronization of only 10% of the neuronal population of the cerebral cortex could produce electrical activity of the magnitude commonly recorded in the EEG. As there are 5 to 10 billion neurons in the cerebral cortex

(Griffith, 1971), this estimate would suggest that the pacemaker neurons could synchronize between ½ and 1 billion neurons at any one time.

It should be recognized that the proposed model does not stand or fall on Andersen and Andersson's work. Rather, the critical ingredient in the model is the concept of a pacemaker or group of pacemaker neurons exerting control over large numbers of cortical neurons via their synaptic junctions. This pacemaker may have its locus in the thalamus as Andersen and Andersson suggest, or it may lie elsewhere. The effect in either case would be the same.

The Mechanism of Central Timing

The proposed mechanism is simple. The thalamic pacemaker neurons discharge periodically and in synchrony. The effect of their activity is felt at the level of the cerebral cortex as a secretion of neural transmitter at numerous synaptic junctions over the entire cortex. Activity in pre-synaptic neurons arising from sensory stimulation also results in the secretion of transmitter substance at these same junctions. Whenever the latter effect occurs in close temporal proximity with the activity of the pacemaker neurons, a sufficient amount of neural transmitter would become available at the synapses to discharge the post-synaptic neurons. In this respect, the transmitter substance produced by activity of the thalamic pacemaker neurons may be thought of as serving the role of a "gate" for controlling the time of discharge of the post-synaptic neurons. The idea of a synaptic transmitter functioning as a gate in neural transmission is not new — Grossberg (1984) employed it in his model of behavior.

In the simple model diagramed in Figure 6, neuron b is one of the pacemaker neurons originating in the thalamus and terminating at a synapse in the cerebral cortex. Neural transmitter is generated at this synapse when neuron b is discharged. Neuron c_1, which also terminates on the same synapse, also generates transmitter substance when it discharges. If both of these neurons discharge at the same time, the transmitter substance from the two sources combined is sufficient to discharge neuron a and elicit a response from E. It is assumed, of course, that neuron a is biased in such a way that, for most conditions, activity of either neuron b or c_1 alone will not produce sufficient neural transmitter to discharge neuron a.

According to this conception of central timing, the EEG as observed on the scalp would become the electrical event associated with the secretions of neural transmitter produced by the activity of the pacemaker neurons. Each peak and/or trough in the rhythmic waves would correspond to the secretion of a unit quantity of neural transmitter. While clearly speculative, this concept is not so difficult to reconcile with present-day knowledge of neurophysiology which treats the EEG as representing the post-synaptic potentials from large numbers of cortical neurons. As the thalamic pacemaker neurons project diffusely to synaptic junctions over the entire cortex, we should expect that the EEG would be recorded in widespread distribution over much of the scalp. Common knowledge confirms this expectation.

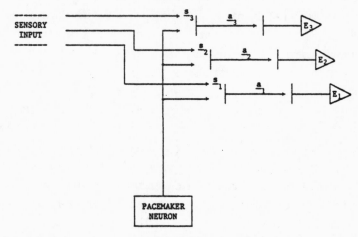

Figure 8: Diagrammatic representation of the physiological basis of central timing.

In Figure 8, a_1, a_2, and a_3 are just 3 of the ½ to 1 billion cortical neurons whose firing is thought to be synchronized by the pacemaker neurons. The electrical activity arising at the synapses, s_1, s_2, and s_3, would be the contribution of these 3 units to the EEG. Figure 8 raises some interesting speculations. As we already noted, it has been suggested that the EEG originates from the post-synaptic potentials of a very large number of synaptic junctions that have been activated simultaneously. In the context of the present model, this activation arises from the firing of the pacemaker neurons. But as shown in Figure 8, the sensory input impinges on these very same synaptic junctions as well. Would not a periodic, rhythmic stimulus that is strong enough to activate a large number of synaptic junctions be expected also to elicit similar post-synaptic potentials? And would not the end result of this be a pattern of activity like that seen in the EEG? In other words, if the model correctly describes the events taking place, it should not matter by what route the synaptic junctions are activated.

We believe there is some evidence which suggests that this may indeed be the case. The evidence concerns the effect of high-intensity, repetitive photic stimulation on the EEG. It is well-known that when a strobe light is flashed in the range of 5-30 flashes per sec, a phenomenon referred to as "photic driving" usually takes place. This consists of the appearance of rhythmic, electrical activity over the posterior regions of the head. The activity is time-locked to the stimulus and is of a frequency identical with or harmonically related to the flash rate.

In a majority of cases, photic driving occurs at or around the frequency of the person's own alpha activity or posterior-dominant rhythm. For this reason, the EEG activity elicited during photic stimulation looks very much like an exceptionally well-regulated alpha rhythm. Our contention is that the phenomenon of photic driving is produced by a mechanism similar to that already proposed for generating the brain's spontaneous rhythmic electrical activity. If this interpretation were indeed correct, a hitherto unexplained phenomenon would have received a simple explanation.

Experimental evidence in support of the EEG being the physiological manifestation of a central timing mechanism derives from a number of studies in several different areas of investigation. This evidence will be considered in later chapters.

The Concept of Transmission System Excitability

Transmission system excitability is more a fact than a concept. It is well-known that neurons go through a cycle following stimulation in which excitability varies over a wide range from absolute refractoriness at one extreme to supra-excitability at the other. It is also recognized that neuronal excitability can be modified by certain drugs and chemicals. Yet, there have been few efforts to incorporate in a systematic way the concept of transmission system excitability into a model of behavior.

The existence of an excitability cycle in neuronal tissue is important for the present model of simple behavior as it provides another means whereby the effector response may be modulated. This will be apparent from an examination of Figure 5. If the excitability of neuron a is heightened (and its threshold correspondingly decreased)—as through the effects of some drug or chemical—the discharge frequency of the neuron will be increased which in turn increases the intensity of the effector response. On the other hand, if the excitability of neuron *a* is depressed, sufficient neural transmitter may not be produced at the synapse to exceed the threshold and neuron *a* may not discharge at all.

A related situation occurs when neuron *a* is refractory from the effects of a previously-occuring stimulus. The consequences of this condition are felt when stimuli are closely-spaced in time. Thus, if a second stimulus follows the first so closely in time that neuron *a* is in a refractory state, it may not discharge in response to the second stimulus. As a result, the effector will fail to respond a second time. Or if neuron *a* only partially recovers its excitability, it would respond but with increased latency so that the effector's response would be delayed. Some of the behavioral consequences of variations occurring in transmission system excitability are taken up in later chapters.

Suppression of Neural Activity — The Concept of Inhibition

Inhibition is a concept of major importance for any theory dealing with behavior. Its history illustrates the interplay of ideas and cross-fertilization of concepts that sometimes takes place between the areas of physiology and psychology. The history of inhibition is of particular interest since the existence of certain behavioral phenomena almost demanded the existence of some physiological mechanisms of inhibition even before they were discovered.

The concept of inhibition appears in early 19th century thought, primarily in the theoretical work of Herbart (see Boring, 1950). Discarded for many years, the concept reappeared when Ebbinghaus used it to explain some of the phenomena that emerged from his historic investigations of memory. By the early 20th century, we find that inhibition was playing a major role in the conditioned reflex theory of Pavlov and in Freud's "repression." All these developments, of course, predate most of our modern knowledge of the physiology of inhibition. At that time, inhibition was considered to be simply a by-product of excitation.

But Pavlov's psychological analysis of conditioning showed that inhibitory phenomena could not be accounted for solely in terms of excitatory principles. It was not until much later, however, that Eccles' (1953) original investigations of the events occurring at the synapse made it clear that inhibition is an active process. This work showed that, while excitation is associated with depolarization, inhibition is a process of hyperpolarization that takes place at the synapse — a phenomenon in its own right and not merely some kind of by-product of excitation. The concept that inhibition is electrically the opposite of excitation, and that neurons can act as inhibitory as well as excitatory devices, lends considerable flexibility to model building in psychophysiology. But more about this later.

CHAPTER 4

PROLONGING NEURAL ACTIVITY—
SOME SIMPLE NEURAL MODELS

EVERY INFORMATION processing system, whether a computer or the brain of a living organism, needs some means of holding onto information until it is used. An information storage system or "memory" can be of three different types depending upon the length of time for which information is stored. The simplest type of storage system is the short-term memory. In such a system, information is held, on-line as it were, until it is used to complete a processing cycle that is currently underway. Next, there is the intermediate memory. In this type of storage system, material is retained for more than immediate use; but the information does not become a part of a person's (or a computer's) working memory. The third type of storage system is the long-term memory. Information that is used over and over again or data that are essential for the smooth and efficient functioning of the information processing system are usually placed into long-term storage.

Either of these three systems can be thought of as prolonging a particular pattern of neural activity until such time when the information represented therein is ready to be used. In the human brain, the short-, intermediate-, and the long-term storage systems appear to be capable of storing the same kind of information. An example of this is the storage of telephone numbers. The number that a person has just looked up in the telephone book prior to dialing is obviously held in short-term storage as it is promptly forgotten. A number used on several occasions in the course of a brief interval of time frequently will be dialed from memory but then will be forgotten. This contrasts with a person's own telephone number which is brought to mind again and again and becomes a permanent part of one's repertoire. Our primary interest in the present work will be with the short-term and intermediate types of memory.

33

Single Chain of Neurons

If we assume that neurons and synapses are the only elements present in the human information processing and transmission system, then the simplest way of storing information for short periods of time is by the use of a circuit consisting of a number of neurons connected together in a single chain. A circuit of this type employing four neurons (d_1, d_2, d_3, and d_4) is shown in Figure 9. The circuit functions like a delay-line and neural activity is prolonged or stored by virtue of the fact that it takes time for an impulse to travel the length of each neuron and to cross each synapse. If we assume that it takes in the neighborhood of 1 msec to traverse a neuron and cross a synapse, then the circuit in Figure 9 will be capable of holding neural activity in store for approximately 4 msec. This is seen in the timing diagram of Figure 9 which shows that 4 msec elapses between the time the spike occurs in neuron c_2 and a spike is emitted by d_4.

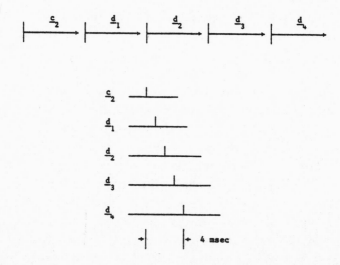

Figure 9: Circuit and timing relationships for a chain of neurons functioning as a delay-line type of short-term memory.

Longer delays, of course, are made possible by adding one or more neurons to the chain. But even very short storage times require a large number of neurons. Unless the time taken to cross the synapses were significantly lengthened, about 1,000 neurons would be needed in the chain to achieve a delay of only 1 sec. At that rate, roughly 3 million such circuits would tie up half the neurons in the cerebral cortex. For this reason, the single chain of neurons—if it is indeed employed by the brain as a storage device—is almost certainly used only as a short-term memory of very limited duration.

Multiple Chain of Neurons with Read-Out

The circuit considered in the last section suffers another limitation. As it stands, the circuit has no flexibility in regard to storage time. Thus, the impulse stored becomes accessible only after it has traversed the entire chain. For this reason, the circuit in Figure 9 is only useful as a limited-access, fixed-duration memory. This limitation can be remedied by adding an additional branch to the axon of each neuron and connecting the neurons in a multiple chain that converges upon another neuron. Such a circuit is seen in Figure 10. This circuit shows the 4 neurons (d_1, d_2, d_3, and d_4) converging upon a single synapse with neuron e. By adding neuron b and suitably biasing neuron e so it fires only when two neurons converging on the synapse are active at nearly the same time, the impulse can be "read out" of storage when neuron b becomes active. This is seen in the timing diagram of Figure 10.

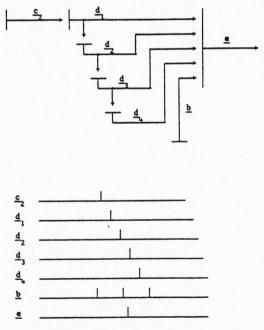

Figure 10: Circuit and timing diagram for a short-term memory consisting of a multiple chain of neurons with gating signal read-out.

Neuron *b* in Figure 10 will be recognized as the gating neuron that was discussed in Chapter 3. The gating neuron makes the impulse held in storage available at a particular time as determined by other events going on in the brain rather than by the delay or total storage time of the circuit. To function in this way, the inter-gate interval — or time between consecutive gating signals — must be equal to or slightly shorter than the delay time of the chain of neurons. If it is not, there will be times when none of the spikes from the *d* neurons come in close proximity to spikes from neuron *b* with the result that the impulse held in storage is lost. The existence of multiple chains of neurons in the central nervous system is well established. Lorente de Nó (1938, 1939) referred to the multiple chain of neurons as one of the two fundamental types of circuit that is systematically repeated in the central nervous system.

Closed Chain of Neurons or Reverberating Circuit

A closed chain of neurons or reverberating circuit is the second of the two fundamental types of circuit referred to by Lorente de Nó. Reverberating circuits provide a more efficient way of storing information for short periods of time than the open chains of neurons. A reverberating circuit consists of two neurons connected together in an arc so that one neuron feeds back on the other. Such a circuit is shown in Figure 11. The circuit is self-exciting in that once neuron m_1 is fired by c_2, the activity in m_1 can be maintained for a time *independently* of any further action by c_2. This is accomplished by f_1, the feed-back neuron which alternately

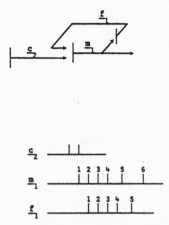

Figure 11: Diagram and timing relationships for a simple reverberating circuit employed as a short-term memory.

fires m_1 or is itself fired by m_1. Such circuits have been called "rever-berating arcs" or "closed self-reexciting chains," and Lorente de Nó (1938) used them to explain how a neural process initiated in a particu-lar area of the brain could propagate itself.

Figure 11 also shows the timing relationships in the simple rever-berating circuit. The process begins with neuron c_2 being discharged by activity in some receptor—the spikes shown here and in the other two tracings represent volleys of impulses. Shortly thereafter, c_2 fires neuron m_1, triggering the spikes numbered 1 and 2. The activity in m_1, in turn, triggers spikes numbered 1 and 2 in feedback neuron f_1—also after a de-lay. These delays represent conduction time of the neuron plus synaptic delay. Once the feedback neuron has become activated it can prolong the activity in m_1. Thus, as shown in Figure 11, spikes 1 and 2 in f_1 trigger spikes 3 and 4 in m_1. The latter, in turn, trigger spikes 3 and 4 in f_1. But now the refractory period of neuron m_1 begins to play a role. Spike 3 in f_1 fails to trigger a response because m_1 is refractory. By the time spike 4 comes along in f_1, however, m_1 has recovered and spike 5 is triggered in m_1. The latter triggers spike 5 in f_1 which, in turn, triggers spike 6 in m_1. The delay in the appearance of spike 6 in neuron m_1 is due to the delayed recovery and hence increased threshold resulting from the passage of the previous impulses.

As the impulses traverse the arc again and again, the thresholds of the two neurons become higher and higher until finally conduction ceases. For this reason, the simple reverberating circuit is able to pro-long activity for only a short time. With a long chain of feedback neurons, i.e., one with many neurons in series, the rate of circulation is reduced and may become low enough to allow activity to be prolonged for considerable periods of time (Lorente de Nó, 1938). Thus, the longer the feedback loop, the greater the period of time for which the activity can be prolonged.

Because the neurons in the closed chain are fired over and over again, the reverberating circuit is more economical in its use of compo-nent elements than the open chain circuit that was considered earlier. As in the case of the open circuit, an additional branch from the axon of each neuron in the chain may be brought out to the synapse of another neuron. This is shown in Figure 12, where the four feedback neurons (f_1, f_2, f_3, and f_4) converge upon neuron e. By adding neuron b and biasing neuron e so it will fire only when two neurons converging on the synapse are active at nearly the same time, the impulse in storage may be "read out" whenever neuron b becomes active. The timing diagram in Figure

12 shows that the impulse in storage can be retrieved again and again at
the time that neuron *b* is active. This differs from the open chain circuit
in Figure 10 in which case the impulse can be retrieved only once after
which it is lost. We see then that the closed-chain circuit can serve as a
short-term memory of longer duration than an open-chain circuit having the same number of neurons in the chain.

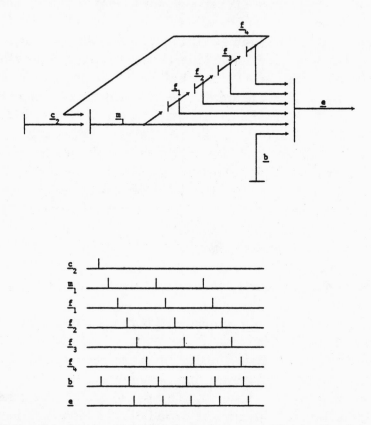

Figure 12: Reverberating circuit with four feedback neurons and gating signal read-out used
as a short-term memory.

A reverberating circuit provides a memory that is wholly a function of
the neural activity going on, independent of any structural change. The
circuit in Figure 12 has some interesting properties. How soon a spike can
be read out after it is first put into storage depends upon where in the gating cycle the spike in c_2 happens to fall. If, as in Figure 12, the spike in
neuron c_2 occurs slightly after a spike has gone by in neuron *b*, read-out will
be minimally delayed by the time it takes the next spike to come along in *b*.
The same, of course, is true of the multiple-chain circuit of Figure 10.

How often a spike in the reverberating circuit may be read out of storage depends upon the frequency of occurrence of the gating signal. Thus, for example, if in Figure 12 the frequency of occurrence of spike b were cut in half, spikes 2, 4, and 6 in neuron b would be absent and the spike in storage would be retrieved only twice during the same interval instead of five times. An even larger reduction in frequency of the gating signal in the multiple-chain circuit could result in a complete failure to retrieve the spike. This happens because the gating signal fails to coincide with the activity in either m_1 or one of the feedback neurons. But if frequency of the gating signal is restored to its previous faster rate, coincidence is once more possible and the spike in storage can again be retrieved. This phenomenon is not an uncommon occurrence in real life; most persons have had the experience of having forgotten something only to discover that they are able to retrieve it from memory moments later.

It will be seen, therefore, that the frequency of the gating signal becomes an important parameter of these circuits. More will be said about this in later chapters.

Inhibitory and Facilitory Loops

One problem with the reverberating circuit in Figure 12 is that other, later-occurring inputs coming over neuron c_2 can interfere with the material presently in storage. This problem may be corrected by the use of an inhibitory loop. By adding another branch to the axons of $m_1, f_1, f_2, f_3,$ and f_4, and terminating these branches on the synapse of an inhibitory neuron that is connected to the synapse of neuron c_2, the effects of any interfering inputs may be eliminated. A circuit of this kind is seen in Figure 13, where i is the inhibitory neuron. Note that, in order to retain the same output relations, neuron e must be biased so it will fire only when four neurons converging on the synapse are active at nearly the same time.

If a spike is fed back into the input of a reverberating circuit each time one is read out, it is possible to reinforce the activity already present in the circuit. Such an arrangement is shown in Figure 14 where neuron r serves as the facilitory, feedback linkage. Note that activity in neuron m_1 will be reinforced whenever spikes are simultaneously present in neurons f_4 and r. According to the timing diagram in Figure 14, this happens once every three times that the reverberating loop is traversed. Under such conditions, the activity already present in the circuit is reinforced for one cycle out of every three cycles.

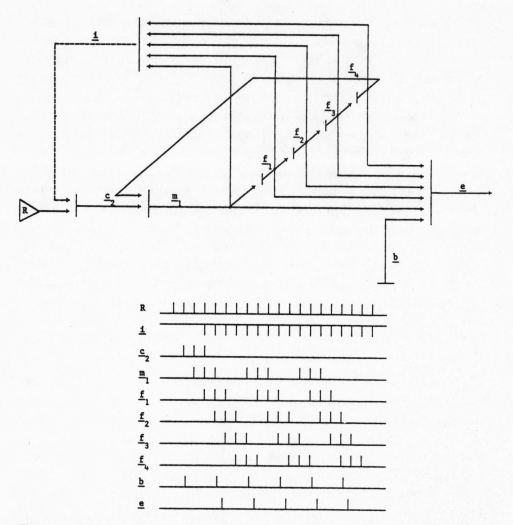

Figure 13: Circuit of Figure 12 with inhibitory feedback loop to·prevent interference from other inputs.

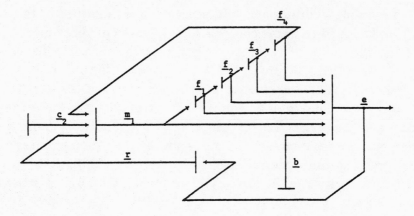

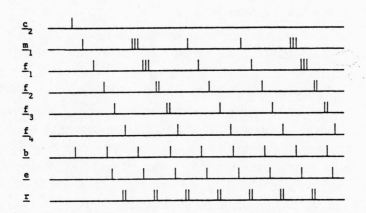

Figure 14: Reverberating circuit of Figure 12 with facilitory feedback loop to reinforce memory in the absence of afferent support.

The simple facilitory and inhibitory devices described in this section serve to lessen some of the concerns that have been voiced in the past regarding the value of reverberating circuits as memory devices—see, e.g., Hebb (1949), Milner (1970). Addition of the facilitory feedback loop serves to keep the cycle of activity going in the absence of any afferent support. In so doing, it provides for storage intermediate between short- and long-term. At the same time, the inhibitory loop prevents other, later inputs coming over the same channel from interferring with and confusing the material already in storage. Configurations of elements like those used in Figures 13 and 14 are known to exist in the brain (Eccles, 1973; Lorente de Nó, 1938, 1939). The proposed circuits, therefore, are not in disharmony with our fundamental knowledge of the architectonics of the central nervous system.

Retrieval from Memory and the Concept of Attention—A Hypothesis

The concept of central timing is an important characteristic and the gating neuron an essential part of the memory circuits considered thus far in the present chapter. Indeed, read-out of the material in storage is controlled by the gating signal. As the circuits stand, neuron b is permanently connected to neuron e, the output neuron, and read-out will occur every time that a gating signal is generated within the brain. In behavioral terms this means that, if material can be retrieved, it will be retrieved from storage over and over again regardless of the needs of the organism. But we know that, under normal conditions, this does not happen. Retrieval is a conditional or optional event. Material stored in even short-term memory *may be* recalled; it does not *have to be* recalled. In other words, the retrieval of information from storage is not an automatism but a process that normally occurs when one's attention is brought to a focus. Retrieval can also take place when the mind wanders; but in this case it appears that information is idly read out from various sources purely at random.

At this point, we take a conceptual leap and make a bold assumption. We hypothesize that focusing the attention is, in physiological terms, equivalent to bringing the gating signal to bear on some specific neural circuit or group of circuits. In short, the circuits shown in Figures 10, 12, 13, and 14 have only the *potential* for being read out. Actual read-out occurs solely when a gating signal is in fact present in neuron b—which happens only when the attention is turned in the direction of these circuits.

This may occur through an act of volition or by chance as a random event. In other words, a gating signal may be selectively connected to some specific neural circuits when a person is attending to a particular task or activity, or randomly connected to any circuit when the mind wanders.

The present hypothesis has some important implications for the functioning of the neural circuits dealt with in this chapter. In the case of the circuit in Figure 10, retrieval from storage cannot take place unless the circuit becomes the focus of attention during the time that the spike traverses the chain. The same is also true of the circuits in Figures 12 and 13; but since a spike can traverse the chain in these circuits more than once, retrieval may occur more than one time. How long a spike can be retained in storage by these circuits depends upon the number and characteristics of the neurons in the chain. As is the case with the circuit in Figure 10, duration of storage in these circuits is independent of retrieval. The circuit in Figure 14 differs in this respect because retrieval from storage is accompanied by reinforcement. Nevertheless, after read-out takes place, the attention may shift away thereby withdrawing the gating signal and leaving the circuit to its own devices. Under such conditions, reverberation in the circuit will ultimately cease unless the attention is once again turned in its direction so that retrieval and reinforcement may occur.

Storing and Retrieving Complex Patterns of Neural Activity

One serious limitation of the memory circuits we have considered thus far is that all of them are able to read out only a single unit of information in a retrieval cycle. This limitation is not immediately apparent in the circuits of Figures 10 and 12 because in these circuits only a single unit of information—one spike—was placed into storage. Thus, in the illustrations given, only a single spike is found at c_2, the input of these circuits. Such being the case, we would expect only one spike to be read out.

But now what happens when a number of spikes—or a *pattern* of neural activity—appears at the input of these circuits? Just such a situation is seen in Figure 13. Here we find 3 spikes present at the input and all 3 of them are placed into storage. As the spikes traverse the circuit, this particular pattern of neural activity is duplicated in m_1 and in each of the feedback neurons. Note in the timing diagram of Figure 13, that spikes corresponding to the 3 input spikes are simultaneously present at the synapse of neuron e by the time feedback neuron f_2 first becomes active.

Turning now to the retrieval cycle, we find — after a gating signal comes along and retrieval occurs — that the pattern of neural activity is not preserved. Only a single spike is read out for the 3 spikes placed into storage. Indeed, the time interval over which the original 3 spikes were spread out has been compressed so that, upon retrieval, the 3 spikes are summed together. This limitation derives from the fact that the circuit has no device for decoding information compressed in the time domain. But it is doubtful that the brain employs any such decoding devices. It is more likely that, from input to final output, the brain's information processing system operates in real time. As it stands, therefore, this type of circuit is of limited value. It could be used as a short-term memory only if a single spike were placed into storage, or if the information contained in a series of spikes were so redundant that transmission beyond the 1st or 2nd spike would become unnecessary.

The multiple-chain circuit of Figure 10 also is found to suffer the same limitation when several spikes are placed in storage. Careful study of the method of storage used in all these circuits reveals that, although a pattern of neural activity is in fact present, it cannot readily be retrieved on demand. The method stores the entire pattern of neural activity at some time in each neuron of the chain. This means that to read out the pattern from beginning to end, in the precise manner in which it was originally laid down, it is necessary to hook up to one of these neurons. But to which neuron and when? By what means will the hook-up be made; and how will its duration be controlled? If the hook-up is made to the wrong neuron, or is made too early or too late, the information may be read out before or after the brain needs it for a particular processing cycle. Or it may only partially be read out.

The answer to these queries is simply that we don't know. Because the material in these circuits is placed into storage without reference to any temporal point of reference within the brain, the brain has no way of telling when the pattern of neural activity will be available in a particular neuron for retrieval. It is apparent, therefore, that with such a storage system retrieval will be controlled by chance and the storage circuit's parameters rather than by the brain's central processing system as it ought to be. The outcome of such an arrangement certainly would be chaotic. In even the simplest forms of behavior, information in short-term storage needs to be made available at a particular time in a processing cycle — either for purposes of comparing it with other information or because it serves as a link in a processing chain.

The foregoing discussion highlights the importance of having some kind of central timing device to control the storage of information as well as its retrieval. It also points the way to a possible solution of the problem at hand. The solution involves using a different and somewhat more complex system of storage in which each single unit of information is read into a separate neuron. Each of these neurons, in turn, is connected to its own short-term storage circuit. In this way, each individual element in a pattern of neural activity becomes stored in a separate circuit, with the first element going into circuit a, the next into circuit b, and so on. The whole assembly of circuits, namely circuits a, b, c, d, ..., constitutes the short-term memory. The process of reading information into and retrieving information from this assembly of circuits is under the control of the gating signal. How this may be carried out is best described by referring to an actual example.

Figure 15 is a circuit for the type of short-term memory we have been considering. The circuit consists of an assembly of identical circuits designated by the letters a, b, and c. Each will be recognized as a multiple-chain memory circuit of the type that was taken up earlier in this

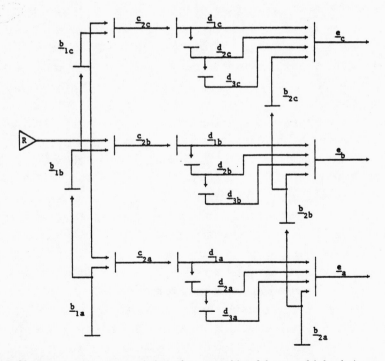

Figure 15: Short-term memory consisting of an assembly of three multiple-chain memory circuits with read-in and read-out under gating signal control.

chapter. Although the assembly consists of only 3 such circuits, it is readily apparent that it could be composed of a much larger number. Similarly, only three d neurons are shown in the chain of each memory circuit; but in practice there could be many of them.

The input of each circuit in the assembly is connected to the source of the signal to be placed into short-term storage. In the present instance, connection is directly to a receptor. But the presence of a spike at the input does not mean that the c_2 neurons will be activated. Spikes appearing at the input have to be "read in" by b_1, the gating signal. To accomplish this, the gating signal itself is put into short-term storage. As Figure 15 shows, a multiple-chain memory circuit is employed for this purpose. Note that the gating signal, designated b_{1a}, goes directly to c_{2a}, the input of the first circuit in the assembly. The axons of the other b_1 neurons in the gating signal storage circuit are connected in consecutive order to the other c_2 neurons. Thus, b_{1b} goes to c_{2b}, b_{1c} to c_{2c}, and so on until a gating signal is made available at the input of every circuit in the assembly.

Information is read in as follows: The process begins with the occurrence of a gating signal in b_{1a} and the consequent appearance of a spike at the synapse of c_{2a}. If a spike originating from activity in R is also present, neuron c_{2a} will be fired thereby placing a spike into storage. The same process takes place at the input of each circuit in the assembly. Note, however, that the gating signal does not appear at the same time in each circuit of the assembly but is delayed by the conduction time plus synaptic delay of each b_1 neuron. The end result is that the short-term memory circuit appears to scan the output of the receptor. If a spike happens to be present at the output of the receptor when a particular branch of the assembly passes by, the spike is captured and placed into storage; if not, the storage circuit of that branch remains empty. In this way, the pattern of neural activity appearing in R may be preserved.

The process of reading information out of the circuit in Figure 15 follows a similar plan. The d neurons in each circuit of the assembly converge upon the synapse of an e neuron. The gating signal is used to control read-out in the same way as it was used to control read-in. Thus, gating signal b_{2a} is run to e_a, the e neuron of "a" circuit in the assembly. Consecutive branches from the gating signal storage circuit—that is, b_{2b}, b_{2c}, etc.—are connected, in turn, to e_b, e_c, etc. Retrieval of a pattern of neural activity from storage consists of reading out the contents of the "a" circuit into neuron e_a, "b" circuit into e_b, and so on until all the circuits in the assembly have been scanned.

Of course, the circuit in Figure 15 suffers the same limitations characteristic of memory circuits employing open, multiple chains of neurons. Because neural activity in such circuits cannot be prolonged beyond the delay time of the open chain of neurons, the retrieval cycle in Figure 15 must follow directly after the read-in cycle. Thus, retrieval will always occur one gating signal after the material has been read into storage. To make this explicit, the gating signal for read-in is designated b_1 and for read-out, b_2. Figure 16 shows the timing relations of the various events that take place in such a circuit when a pattern of neural activity consisting of spike, blank, spike is placed into storage. In this illustration, the "a," "b," and "c" circuits each contain 17 d neurons instead of 3 as in Figure 15. The pattern of neural activity appearing at the input is retrieved one gating signal later in neurons e_a, e_b, and e_c. Note that the time relations of the original signal are preserved.[1]

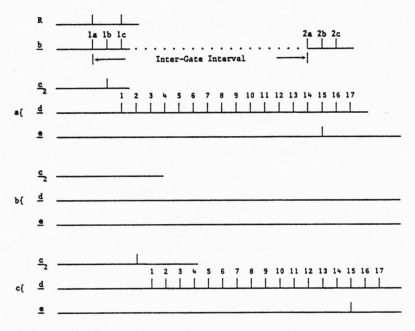

Figure 16: Timing diagram for the short-term memory circuit in Figure 15 with seventeen d neurons in each branch.

---

[1]It should be recognized that b_1 and b_2, the first and second gating signals, are not selectively connected to input and output of the circuit shown in Figure 15. All gating signals go to the c_2 and e neurons alike. This means, of course, that the processes of storage and retrieval can occur simultaneously. As shown in the timing diagram (Figure 16), the circuit in the illustration with 17 d neurons in each branch stores information on one cycle and retrieves it on the next.

In order to overcome the limitations imposed by using open, multiple chains of neurons as storage elements, closed chains of neurons may be substituted in the circuit of Figure 15. The result of doing this is seen in Figure 17 where 3 reverberating memory circuits have been exchanged for the multiple chain circuits. As a whole, the circuit functions in the same manner as the short-term memory circuit in Figure 15. The only difference between the two is that the reverberating circuits allow information to be retained in storage for longer periods of time. This means that retrieval from storage is not limited to the single cycle immediately following the read-in cycle, but may occur more than once and at different times. For this reason, the gating signal serving to retrieve information from the circuit is designated b_{1+n} in Figure 17, where $n = 1$, 2, 3, etc. Aside from providing added flexibility of retrieval, this circuit has the advantage of making more efficient use of the neurons employed in the storage process.

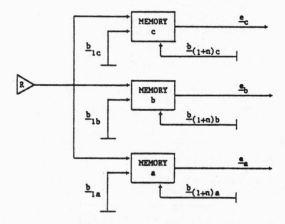

Figure 17: Short-term memory consisting of an assembly of three reverberating memory circuits — a, b, and c — with read-in and read-out under gating signal control.

Storage Capacity

While this chapter is not intended to be an exhaustive inquiry into the topic of brain memory circuits, we can hardly leave the topic without touching on the matter of storage capacity. How much information an assembly of memory circuits like the one in Figure 17 can store at any one time is limited primarily by the number of separate circuits in the assembly. But there are other considerations. Whenever storage capacity of such an assembly exceeds the time that elapses between any 2 gating signals occurring at read-in time, double-entry into storage may occur. To avoid this and the resultant confusion, the second of the 2 gating signals has to be suppressed. Such suppression may be achieved by the use of an inhibitory loop similar to that taken up earlier in this chapter.

For prolonging longer trains of information, several circuits of the type shown in Figure 17 can be connected together in series. The first would be activated by b_1, and the 2nd by b_2, and so on. In this way, information appearing during each gating cycle would be stored in a separate assembly with each assembly being keyed to the order of the gating signals. Retrieval from storage in such a system would follow a similar pattern. But matters such as these are concerned more with the area of complex behavior which is outside the scope of the present work.

Conclusions

In this chapter, we have discussed some of the ways in which information may be stored for short periods of time, assuming that the basic building blocks of a short-term memory system are neurons and synapses. Given our current knowledge concerning the functioning of neurons and synapses, it is relatively easy to construct some simple circuits for prolonging neural activity. However, problems arise when we consider the question of how stored information gets retrieved and integrated into behavior. The need in even the simplest behavior to scan patterns of neural activity in memory, retrieve selected patterns, and enter them smoothly into the flow of ongoing behavior suggests that information storage and retrieval must be under the control of some central timing mechanism. Because scanning by its very nature is a cyclic process, it is difficult to conceive of an information storage and retrieval system in which the scanning is not controlled by some kind of periodically-occurring timing or gating signal.

In Chapter 3, it was suggested that the spontaneous, rhythmic electrical activity of the brain is the physiological basis of the central timing mechanism hypothesized to control the brain's information-processing circuits. There appears to be no reason why this same electrical activity should not serve the same function for the brain's memory circuits as well. Additionally, we have hypothesized that the process of focusing the attention is equivalent, in physiological terms to bringing the gating signal to bear on some specific neural circuit or circuits. It will be seen, therefore, that the concept of central timing is destined to play a major role in the rest of our inquiry.

CHAPTER 5

A MODEL OF SIMPLE REACTION TIME

IN THE PRESENT CHAPTER, the elements in the model of simple behavior and the concepts that were taken up in the last two chapters will be combined into a model of simple reaction time (RT). We begin with the simplest case of simple RT. This is the case where (1) all signals impinging on R, the receptor, are the same, (2) all signals are imperative stimuli, and (3) none of the signals are closely spaced in time—so that the effects of any one signal are independent of the effects of any signals coming before. Conditions (1) and (2) imply, of course, that there is no noise in the signal environment. In addition, we suppose that the attention is steadily fixed on the task, shifting away only momentarily when a response is elicited.

Anatomy of the Model — the Simplest Case

Let us consider a specific example in which an auditory signal, say a pure tone, is the stimulus. In the typical experiment, many such signals may be presented during the course of a test session. The tones are all well above the threshold of R, are widely spaced in time, and are the only detectable stimuli in the environment. A subject participating in the experiment responds to each tone by contracting a specific muscle or set of muscles as quickly as possible. The model shown in Figure 6 of Chapter 3 provides a mechanism for producing the required responses, assuming that the activity elicited in c_1 by the stimulus occurs in close temporal proximity to a gating signal. Given that the necessary pathways exist and are open at the time of stimulation, the events that take place—from stimulus to response—are straightforward. The diagram in Figure 7 shows the timing relations of these events. The RT, of course, is the time that elapses between the beginning of the stimulus and the initiation of the subject's response.

But a close examination of the effects of various possible stimulus configurations on the circuit in Figure 6 reveals a serious flaw in the model. As the circuit stands, no response would be forthcoming or possible whenever a tone was so short that the activity elicited in c_1 failed to intersect a gating signal. This condition is diagramed in Figure 18. The critical factor in the circuit's failure to elicit a response is the duration of the stimulus in relation to the inter-gate interval (IGI)—the duration of the time interval between consecutive gating signals. Note that, whenever a stimulus is very short in relation to the IGI, the probability of response failure could be quite high. It is well-known that clicks having durations no greater than 1 msec can be adequate stimuli for the human auditory system. As we shall see later, the IGI may vary over a wide range but is considered to be substantially greater than 1 msec. Taking all these factors into account, it is apparent that some device for prolonging a stimulus becomes necessary if the model is to satisfy the demands of reality.

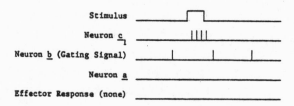

Figure 18: Timing diagram for the circuit shown in Figure 6 when the activity elicited by short-duration stimuli fails to coincide with a gating signal.

The obvious solution to our problem is to add a short-term memory to the circuit. In selecting the proper memory circuit, a number of factors need to be considered. Since RTs measured under the present conditions may be considerably less than 200 msec, and as there is no need to prolong the stimulus beyond the response, a reverberating-type circuit seems unnecessary. Moreover, as mentioned earlier, the stimuli are pure tones and the only signals present in the environment. This being the case, it is only necessary to preserve the actual initiation of the stimulus in storage; whatever follows is redundant as far as present purposes are concerned. For these reasons and in the interest of simplicity, a multiple-chain memory circuit like the one shown in Figure 10 of Chapter 4 is selected.

Figure 19 shows such a multiple-chain memory circuit connected in series with the model of simple RT. The example given in the timing diagram at the bottom of the figure illustrates the outcome when the stimulus occurs slightly ahead of the first gating signal shown. It will be seen that when this happens, the spike in d_1 misses the first gating signal and the response is delayed until the second gating signal comes along. Note, in this connection, that the second gating signal has to occur before the spike goes by in d_n else the stimulus will be lost as far as neuron a is concerned. This means, of course, that the IGI cannot be longer than transmission time through the chain of d neurons and their synapses for the circuit to work.

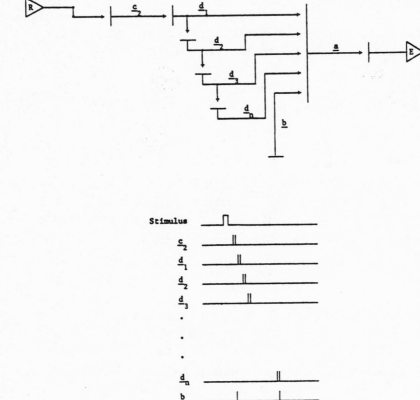

Figure 19: A model of simple reaction time employing a multiple chain of n d neurons as a short-term memory.

For the example given in Figure 19, the RT is slightly longer than the IGI. If the stimulus occurred a little earlier so that the first gating signal would not be missed by d_1, the RT could be considerably shorter. On the other hand, if the subject's attention happened to wander and shift briefly at the time the stimulus was going through storage, the gating signal may not be brought to bear on the circuit at the correct time and no response at all would occur. With even this simple model, therefore, considerable variation in the RT is possible. We will return to the matter of variability in the RT when the psychophysiology of simple RT is taken up in the next chapter.

Although the model diagramed in Figure 19 is useful as a way of illustrating how simple behavior may come about, the simplest case of simple RT is hardly if ever encountered, even in the laboratory. There are a number of reasons for this. First and most important of all is the fact that the environment in which an imperative auditory stimulus usually occurs is not entirely free of other audible signals. These may come from the outside environment or from within the subject himself. If some noise occurred that was sufficient to stimulate R, the system diagramed in Figure 19 would yield a response. Indeed, as this model stands, a response will be elicited by any and all supra-threshold auditory signals that might occur; assuming, of course, that the signals were spaced sufficiently far apart that their effects on the circuit are independent of each other. In order for the model to be of any practical value, therefore, it has to be modified so it can function properly in an environment where other auditory signals besides the actual stimuli might be present.

Noise in the Signal Environment

What happens psychologically when some noise occurs in the environment while the RT is being measured? As anyone who has ever taken part in a RT experiment knows, it is not uncommon for a response to be elicited erroneously. When this happens, we tell the subject that he or she has "jumped the gun" and should make sure next time that it was really the stimulus and not some noise he/she heard before responding. In doing so, we are asking the subject's central nervous system to be more selective, to recognize and filter out the imperative stimulus from other sounds present in the environment. But how does the central nervous system go about doing this? How does it decide that a particular signal is the stimulus when there are other signals around that are not stimuli?

One possibility immediately comes to mind. A sample of standard duration is picked up from the signal environment by the receptor and compared with a sample of the actual stimulus previously stored in memory. Whenever the two samples are found to be reasonably the same, it is concluded that the sample from the signal environment contains the stimulus and a response would be elicited. On the other hand, when the two samples are found to be different, no response would occur. If the samples being compared were no longer in duration than the IGI, a comparison like this could be made every time a gating signal came along. In this way, a decision concerning the presence or absence of a stimulus in a noisy environment could be made for each and every gating cycle.

Design of a Comparator Circuit

In order to compare two samples of neural activity and decide whether they are the same or different, some kind of comparator circuit is essential. With only neurons and synapses to work with, the choice of designs is limited.

In its simplest form, a comparator circuit might consist of two neurons converging on a synapse of a third neuron. Such a circuit is seen in Figure 20. Neurons n_1 and n_2 come together at the synapse of

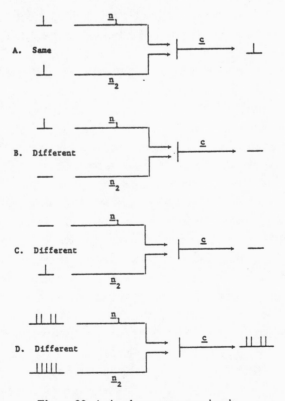

Figure 20: A simple comparator circuit.

neuron c, which is biased so that it fires only when n_1 and n_2 are simultaneously active. As seen in Figure 20A, c fires when the inputs to both neurons are identical — i.e., when spikes are simultaneously present at n_1 and n_2. Figures 20B and 20C show the two possible cases when the inputs are different; note that neuron c is silent in both cases.

The simple comparator circuit functions in a similar fashion when a *pattern* of neural activity instead of a single spike is present at one or both inputs. This is shown in Figure 20D. Note that the output of the neuron c is a pattern of spikes identical to the input with a missing spike.

It will be seen that a comparison between two different samples of neural activity is readily carried out by this circuit. But the question of deciding similarity or difference is another matter. With the input consisting of only a single spike, a decision follows directly from the comparison. In other words, an output in c means that the inputs being compared are alike; no output means that they are different. A problem arises, however, when patterns of neural activity rather than single spikes are compared. Two patterns that are not identical can be different from each other by various degrees. At one extreme they may be almost alike while at the other they could be totally different. In order to make a decision between the two alternatives, some method is needed for estimating the degree of similarity or difference between the two samples being compared. Having obtained such an estimate, this estimate could be compared with some kind of standard — the degree of similarity required or the maximum permissible difference allowed. If this standard was not met, the samples would be judged to be different; if it was, they would be considered the same.

One way of estimating the degree of similarity or difference between two patterns of neural activity is simply to count up the number of times in a sample of standard duration that the two patterns are alike. The resulting quantity could then be compared against a number that represents an acceptable degree of similarity. If this number was not reached, it would be concluded that the two patterns are different. To do this, we require a circuit that can add up the number of times that the two sample patterns of neural activity are alike. Within the limitations imposed by the structural components of the central nervous system, how might such a circuit be designed? We begin, of course, with the output of the comparator circuit (see Figure 20). If the circuit is silent, the two samples of neural activity compared are different. If the circuit is active, the samples are the same. The degree of similarity is proportional to the amount of activity in c, with higher levels of activity present when the samples are more alike. However, the question still remains of how the amount of activity in c can be combined and then compared with a standard so it may be used to make a decision. For this purpose, some kind of integrator circuit is required.

An Integrator Circuit

In our discussion of short-term memory circuits in Chapter 4, an interesting characteristic of these circuits was brought to light. It will be recalled that every spike in a pattern of neural activity placed into storage appears at some time or other in each of the consecutive neurons that form the chain of the memory circuit. All these neurons converge upon a single synapse where spikes corresponding to each of the spikes in the input occur all at the same time. As we noted in the earlier discussion, although the original pattern of neural activity is present, it no longer is spread out over an interval but appears to be compressed in the time domain. From the standpoint of the synapse, neural transmitter from all sources of activity is pooled together. The process is equivalent to summing together or integrating the spikes that appeared in the original pattern of neural activity. If a short-term memory circuit of this type were connected to the output of the comparator, the pattern of neural activity present in the comparator circuit would similarly be integrated.

This is illustrated in Figure 21 for a circuit with five d neurons. Input to this circuit comes from a comparator circuit like that described in the last section. The presence of a spike or spikes at the input means, of course, that the samples of neural activity being compared are alike.

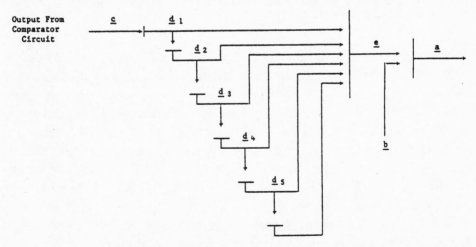

Figure 21: Multiple chain short-term memory circuit used as an integrator. Neuron e, the integrator neuron is biased so it will fire whenever a set number of d neurons is simultaneously active. See Figure 22 for a typical timing diagram.

58   *Psychophysiology*

Figure 22 is a timing diagram for the case in which neuron *e* is biased to fire whenever four or more *d* neurons are active. Let us trace through the operation of this circuit in detail, using the timing diagram.

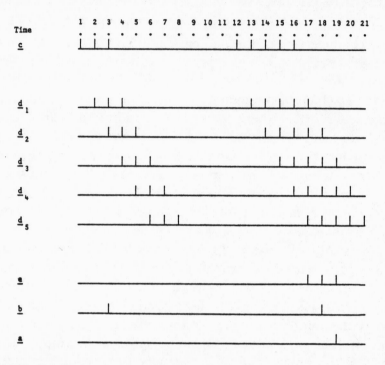

Figure 22: Timing diagram for integrator circuit in Figure 21. Neuron *e* is biased to fire when four or more *d* neurons are simultaneously active. Neuron *a* fires when neurons *e* and *b* are active at nearly the same time.

Starting at time 1, the presence of a spike in neuron *c* indicates that a similarity has been detected between the stimulus stored in memory and the sample picked up from the signal environment. This activity in neuron *c* causes neuron d_1 to fire at time 2 which, in turn, fires neuron d_2 and so on down the line. The spikes in neuron *c* at times 2 and 3 likewise mean that similarities have again been detected by the comparator circuit. These spikes elicit activity in the chain of *d* neurons as well. Note that, at times 4, 5, and 6, spikes elicited by spikes 1, 2, and 3 in neuron *c* are *simultaneously* present at the synapse of neuron *e*. In other words, their effects have been added together. But nothing further happens because neuron *e* is biased to fire only when 4 or more *d* neurons are simultaneously active.

Compare this with what happens when a greater degree of similarity is detected and spikes are present in neuron *c* at times 12, 13, 14, 15, and

16 in Figure 22. Note that four or more of the *d* neurons are simultaneously firing at times 16, 17, and 18 so that neuron *e* fires at time 17 and again at times 18 and 19. As a gating signal appears at time 18, neuron *a* fires at time 19 thus signaling that a stimulus has been detected. If the gating signal did not occur until time 20, it is obvious that neuron *a* would not fire despite the fact that a stimulus nevertheless was detected. However, it will also be obvious that, by adding more *d* neurons to the chain, the fact that a stimulus was indeed detected can be prolonged for an additional time until the gating signal finally comes along.

Anatomy of the Model — The Practical Case

Keeping the material from the last two sections in mind, let us return to our model of simple RT and see how the model can be modified to accomodate the practical problem of noise in the signal environment. When we digressed from our earlier discussion of simple RT, it was suggested that noise could be identified by taking a sample from the signal environment and comparing it with a similar sample of the actual stimulus stored in memory. Depending upon whether these samples were the same or different, a response would or would not be elicited. Using the circuits taken up in the last two sections of this chapter, let us put together a practical model for doing just that.

To begin with, a sample of the actual stimulus will have to be placed into storage. Since we will be dealing with patterns of neural activity, an assembly-type rather than a single-input type of short-term memory circuit will be required. Moreover, as the material in storage will need to be retrieved on demand more than once, a reverberating circuit is necessary. For this reason, the type of circuit shown in Figure 17 is selected for the job. The output of the memory circuit is connected to one side of the comparator circuit, while the receptor is connected to the other side. As seen in Figure 23, the signals from both sources are read simultaneously into the comparator circuit each time a gating signal comes along. In our example, read-in begins with the gating signal designated $b_{1a,b,c,...}$ in Figure 23. The subscripts a, b, c, . . . refer to the consecutive gating signals that are generated by feeding a single gating signal into a multiple-chain, short-term memory circuit. As explained in Chapter 4, the net effect of doing this is that the comparator circuit appears to scan the receptor and memory-circuit outputs simultaneously.

Operation of the comparator and integrator circuits was taken up in detail earlier. If the two samples are judged to be the same according to

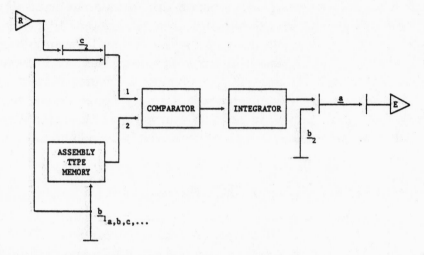

Figure 23: A model of simple RT in which successive samples of the signal environment are compared with a sample of the actual stimulus held in memory.

the criterion employed, the integrator circuit will generate an output. On the other hand, if the samples are judged to be different, no output is produced.

While the circuit in Figure 23 appears somewhat complex in detail, its overall operation is relatively simple. A response will be generated by E, the effector, every time a gating signal comes along *and* there is output from the integrator circuit. This means, of course, that a response is elicited by E when and only when a sample taken from the signal environment is in fact the stimulus. This is exactly the kind of model we have been looking for.

An Alternative Model

An alternative way of dealing with the problem of noise in the signal environment uses a different kind of strategy. Rather than comparing a sample of the signal environment with a sample of the actual stimulus, two consecutive samples taken from the signal environment are compared with each other. One sample comes from the present time, beginning with the current gating signal and lasting the duration of a gating cycle. The other is taken from the immediate past or one gating cycle earlier. Both samples are connected to a comparator circuit like the one described earlier in this chapter. The signal from the past is connected to one side of the circuit, being fed in from short-term memory, while the signal from the present goes to the other side and is fed in on-line.

The principle on which this circuit operates is simple. It is assumed that noise in the signal environment occurs at random and that any signal that is not noise is a stimulus. Based on these assumptions, samples from past and present should differ from each other only by chance — unless an actual stimulus happens to be in one of them. Thus, with only noise in both samples, the comparator circuit will generate an output indicating that there is no difference between the signals past and present. When a stimulus first occurs, it will be picked up by only one side of the comparator circuit. Under these conditions, the output of the comparator circuit is silent.

Figure 24 shows a circuit for the kind of system we have been describing. The receptor is connected to two parallel circuits that are connected, in turn, to the comparator. One of these circuits consists of an assembly-type memory whose output goes to one side of the comparator. The other, which consists only of neuron c_2, goes to the other side. An assembly-type of memory circuit is employed since the model has to recognize patterns of neural activity and not just single spikes. Moreover, because read-out from memory will follow read-in on the next gating signal, a multiple-chain circuit rather than a reverberating type is used. Material is read into storage by the gating signal designated $b_{1a,b,c,\ldots}$, where the subscripts a, b, c, . . . refer to the consecutive gating signals that are generated by feeding a single gating signal into a multiple-chain, short-term memory circuit. The material is read out of storage and into the top half of the comparator circuit on the next gating signal, namely, $b_{2a,b,c,\ldots}$ in Figure 24. At the same time this happens, the signal

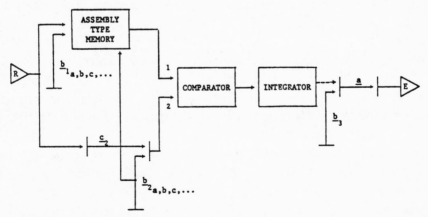

Figure 24: A model of simple RT in which consecutive samples from the signal environment are compared with each other.

from the receptor is read into the bottom half of the comparator circuit. By means of this maneuver, two consecutive samples from the signal environment are made available for comparison.

Operation of the comparator and integrator circuits is the same as was described earlier with one exception. When noise only and therefore no signal is present in the two samples being compared, there will be an output from the integrator. On the other hand, when an actual stimulus is present at the bottom half of the comparator circuit, the output of the comparator circuit and of the integrator circuit as well will be silent. But these outcomes are the opposite of what is required—the circuit we need should elicit a response when the two samples are different, not when they are the same. In other words, the occurrence of a difference should signal that a stimulus has been detected. Fortunately, the concept of inhibition provides a ready solution to the problem. By making the output of the integrator circuit inhibitory, and biasing neuron a so it will fire when one spike is present at the synapse, the outcomes may be reversed. With such an arrangement, activity in b_3 will fire neuron a unless an inhibitory output from the integrator circuit is present at the time.

Comparison of Models

The model we have been discussing differs from the model considered earlier primarily in the method used to identify a stimulus. In the earlier model, samples from the signal environment were compared with a sample of the actual stimulus. Thus, if the stimulus happened to be a 1000 Hz tone, each sample from the signal environment would be compared against a 1000 Hz tone held in storage. If a match failed to be achieved on the first comparison, the comparison could be repeated on the next gating cycle and so on until a match was reached or the stimulus ran out. In so doing, this model makes sure that the signal is really a stimulus before responding. At the same time, it assures that a response will be elicited if a stimulus is indeed present. But the RT in such cases could be quite long since the duration of a gating cycle is consumed by each comparison. For this reason, the operation of this model may be characterized as being "slow but sure."

The operation of the second model is the direct opposite of the first and is characterized as being "fast," but disposed to making errors. In this model, everything that is not noise is considered to be a stimulus. Since noise is assumed to occur at random, samples from the signal environment will differ from each other only by chance. Thus, the model searches for differences in consecutive samples. If a difference is detected, and it exceeds some maximally acceptable difference for noise, the model concludes that a stimulus has occurred and elicits a response. Because nothing is held in storage for longer than a single gating cycle, however, there is little or no opportunity for making a second comparison. If the stimulus happens to be longer than one but shorter than two gating cycles, a second comparison may be possible. But once both sides of the comparator become filled with a stimulus, a response is no longer possible. For this reason we might expect that, compared with the other model, the RTs in the case of this model will be short but also that errors — omitted responses and responses elicited when no actual stimulus is present — will be more frequent.

It is possible that a subject might use both strategies interchangeably in performing a RT task, changing from one to the other depending upon the error rate and his or her own perceptions of response speed. Regardless of which system is used, however, RT will be longer if the attention is not focused upon the task at the time the stimulus occurs. These matters, however, are taken up in the next chapter.

CHAPTER 6

TESTING THE MODELS—THE PSYCHOPHYSIOLOGY OF SIMPLE REACTION TIME

H AVING PROPOSED two models of simple RT, our next task is to examine the models in the context of what we presently know about the phenomenon. In short, we have to find out how well the proposed models fit some of our basic knowledge about RT.

Inferences From the Proposed Models— The Phenomenon of RT Variability

The major dimension that needs to be accommodated by the proposed models is the variability that occurs in the RT. The fact that a person's RT can vary substantially from one trial to another, and that RT may show marked differences between individuals, is well documented (Woodworth, 1938). As far back as the late 18th and early 19th centuries, astronomers recognized that in measuring the time of transit of a star across the meridian, different individuals came up with different results. The procedure they used is not unlike a reaction-time experiment, and for a time it was believed that individuals differed from each other by a fixed amount that could be measured and used in a "personal equation." In this way, it was thought that the transit times of different observers could be brought into harmony. But then, it was discovered that variability occurred *within* individuals as well as *between* individuals; which means, of course, that the personal equation is a variable and not a constant (Bowie, 1913).

Although RT variability has been a frequent topic of theoretical interest in the experimental psychology literature, the phenomenon has not captured the interest of many psychophysiologists. This seems surprising in the light of Rosenblith and Vidale's (1962) "rational assumption" that important changes in the RT reflect information-processing operations in the central nervous system. Factors like flucuations in nerve conduction time and variations in excitability have been suggested and must certainly be involved; but these have not been woven into the fabric of a systematic theory. Indeed, the literature is meager insofar as specific physiological mechanisms are concerned to account for RT variability. Nevertheless, to be of any real value, a psychophysiological model of simple RT must be capable of explaining how the variability in simple RT within an individual comes about, and why some individuals or groups of individuals have longer or shorter RTs than others.

In Chapter 5 it was noted that the responses elicited by the proposed models could display considerable variation in the RT. Let us now return to these models and identify the actual sources of this variability. When this inquiry has been completed, we will address the question of how well RT variability as displayed by the models describes the variability observed in human RT. Finally, some current knowledge about the psychophysiology of simple RT will be surveyed to discover whether this evidence is in accord with the functioning of the models. We assume, as we did in Chapter 5, that the models are functioning under conditions where the stimuli are widely spaced in time. This means that the effects of any one stimulus are independent of the effects of any stimuli coming before.

Sources of RT Variability — The Consecutive-Sample Model

Let us begin by considering the model in which consecutive samples from the signal environment are compared with each other. The circuit for this model is seen in Figure 24 of Chapter 5. It will be recalled from the earlier discussion that any significant differences that are detected between the two samples being compared are attributed to the presence of a stimulus. When this happens, a response is elicited.

One source of variability in the RT of the responses elicited by this model is the temporal location of a stimulus with respect to the gating signals. This is illustrated in Figure 25 which shows in abbreviated form what happens to the RT when stimuli are initiated at different phases of the gating cycle.[1] The shaded areas in the diagrams illustrate the time

---

[1]Note that the diagrams in this and in Figures 26, 27, 28, and 29 show none of the afferent delays that occur between the initiation of the stimulus and the time that the stimulus is fed into the comparator and memory circuits. The diagrams have been abbreviated and simplified in this way for the sake of clarity.

relations that obtain as the stimulus is read into the assembly-type memory and the two inputs of the comparator.

In the upper part of Figure 25, the stimulus is initiated after the second but before the third gating signal in the diagram. The point of interest is the comparison of the signal standing in input 1 of the comparator with that standing in input 2. In the interval between gating signals 1 and 2, no signal is present at either input. Assuming that the noise levels from the environment are the same during this interval and the interval between gating signal 1 and the gating signal immediately preceding it, the inputs are judged to be identical and the comparator

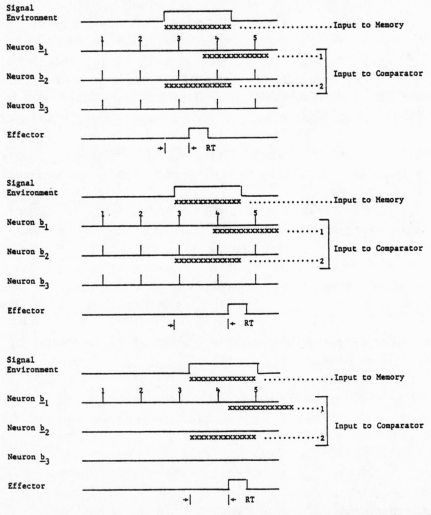

Figure 25: Abbreviated timing diagrams for the Consecutive-Sample Model of simple RT shown in Figure 24 when stimuli are initiated at different phases of the gating cycle.

generates an excitatory output. This signal, thereupon, is converted to an inhibitory output by the integrator, and the inhibitory output prevents neuron b_3, the gating neuron, from firing neuron a and producing a response.

Moving now to the interval between gating signals 2 and 3, we find that input 1 of the comparator still contains no signal but that input 2 shows a signal for part of the time. This difference is sufficiently large so that the two inputs are no longer judged to be the same. As a result, the integrator output is silent and the next gating signal coming along (gating signal 3) fires neuron a and elicits a response. If the amount of signal present at comparator input 2 during this interval were insufficient for the comparator to detect a difference, the circuit would move on to the interval between gating signals 3 and 4. This might happen if some noise occurred during the interval between gating signals 1 and 2. This noise would appear at input 1 of the comparator during the interval defined by gating signals 2 and 3 and could be mistaken as signal. In such a case, the response would be delayed until gating signal 4 came along, and the RT would be prolonged by the duration of a whole inter-gate interval. The middle and lower parts of Figure 25 show how the RT can vary as the temporal location of the stimulus with respect to the gating signal changes. The principles of operation already discussed apply in each of these cases.

In a reaction task where the stimuli are presented at random and without warning, the occurrence of a stimulus bears no temporal relationship to any of the events going on in the circuit or the system to which it belongs. For this reason, the particular phase of a gating cycle in which a stimulus happens to fall is purely up to chance. This means that all the different values of RT that result from differences in the temporal location of the stimulus are equally probable. If no other sources of variability were involved, the distribution of RT generated by this model would be rectangular.

A second source of variability in the RT of the responses displayed by the model we are discussing is the frequency of the gating signals. Figure 26 shows the RT for 3 different frequencies under conditions where the phase of the gating cycle in which the stimulus falls is held constant. It is obvious from Figure 26 that the RT increases as frequency of the gating signal decreases. Likewise it is apparent that if there were two individual models identical in every respect except for the frequency of the gating signal, the individual having the less frequently occurring gating signals, would elicit the longer RT. Less obvious is the fact that, as gating signal frequency decreases, larger portions of the signal environment go into the comparison and decision-making process. Note in the upper part of Figure 26, that less than half the total duration of the stimulus is included in the interval between gating signals 3 and 4 when gating signal frequency is a maximum. When, on the other hand, gating signal frequency is a minimum, as in the diagram at the bottom of Figure 26, nearly twice as much of the stimulus falls within the same interval. Because of this, we might expect that fewer errors would be made in detecting the stimulus when gating signal frequency is low than when it is high.

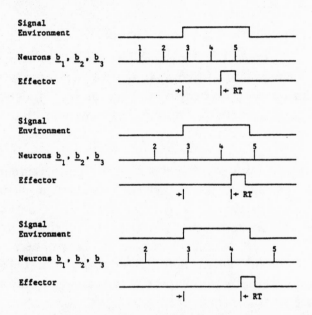

Figure 26: Abbreviated timing diagrams for the Consecutive-Sample Model of simple RT (Figure 24) when frequency of the gating signal is allowed to vary.

Assuming no other sources of variability are involved besides gating signal frequency, the distribution of RT generated by this model could be expected to closely follow the distribution of IGI — the durations between consecutive gating signals. Thus, for example, if the distribution of IGI was normal, we would expect the distribution of RT to be normal as well.

A third source of variability in the responses produced by this model is the excitability of the component elements — the neurons which make up the model. Two major factors that determine excitability at any instant are the previous stimulation to which the circuit has been exposed and the recovery time of the neurons involved. Although we assumed at the outset that our model would only be dealing with stimuli that are widely spaced in time, and, hence would avoid the question, this seldom happens outside the laboratory. Moreover, different individual neurons may display different levels of excitability, either because of inherent structural differences or because of the effects of certain drugs or chemicals. However, because the matter of excitability and recovery from stimulation is a whole topic in itself, it will be dealt with later when the problem of closely-spaced stimuli is taken up.

Sources of RT Variability — The Comparison-With-Standard Model

The reader will remember that, with this model, successive samples of the signal environment are compared with a sample of the actual stimulus held in memory. Whenever the samples are judged to be the same, a response is elicited. A glance at the circuit in Figure 23 shows that the two sources of RT variability that were discussed in the last section apply equally well to the present model. In other words, the temporal position of a stimulus with respect to the gating signals, and the frequency of the gating signal, are both sources of variability in the RT. There is, however, an important difference between the two models. The difference is associated with the fact that, when the stimuli are long enough, the present model can improve the accuracy of detecting a stimulus by taking a second look at the signal environment. This phenomenon was mentioned briefly in Chapter 5. Let us now examine in detail what takes place when this happens.

In Figure 27 we see how this circuit behaves when the temporal location of the stimulus with respect to the gating signals is allowed to vary. The conditions are the same as in Figure 25 for the Consecutive-Sample Model. The diagrams in the middle of Figures 25 and 27 show that both of the proposed models yield identical RTs when the stimulus falls just ahead of a gating signal. Note, in both instances, that the stimulus fills the entire gating cycle that follows.

What happens when the circuit takes a second look at the signal environment is illustrated by the diagram in the lower part of Figure 27. The first comparison is made between the standard and the portion of the signal environment that falls between gating signals 2 and 3. For this comparison, about three-quarters of the gating cycle is filled with the stimulus. If the standard and the sample from the signal environment

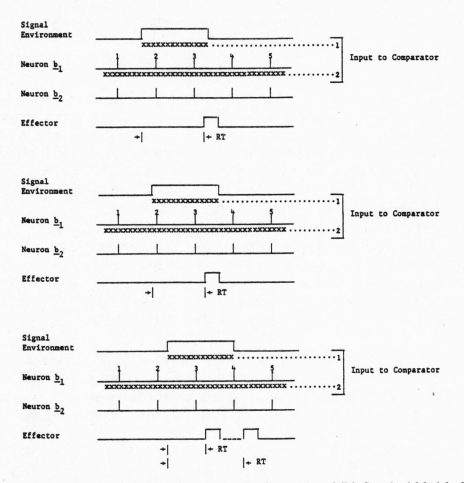

Figure 27: Abbreviated timing diagrams for the Comparison-With-Standard Model of simple RT shown in Figure 23 when stimuli are initiated at different phases of the gating cycle.

are judged to be reasonably the same, a response will be elicited shortly after gating signal 3. But the circuit can make a more conservative decision by taking a second look at the signal environment and comparing the standard with the signal environment that falls between gating signals 3 and 4. In this case, note that the entire gating cycle is filled with the stimulus. The two samples thereupon are judged to be identical and a response is elicited shortly after gating signal 4 — one whole gating cycle later than the response when the less conservative judgment was applied.

The outcome when the same conditions are imposed on the Consecutive-Sample Model is different, and may be seen by examining

the diagram in the lower part of Figure 25. The comparison shown in
the diagram is made between the samples marked off by gating signals 3
and 4. Note that the two samples are judged to be different from each
other and a response is elicited shortly after gating signal 4 as seen in the
diagram. In the event that this response were withheld and a second
comparison was made, the portion of the stimulus between gating
signals 4 and 5 would move to the comparator. In this instance, the samples compared are nearly the same—i.e., the stimulus is present for
75% of the interval in input 1 and 100% in input 2. The result is an excitatory output from the comparator which, in turn, causes the integrator to produce an inhibitory output. The net effect is that no response
would be elicited even though a stimulus is in fact present.

Thus, while a second comparison increases the accuracy of responding in the case of the Comparison-With-Standard Model, it can result in
no response at all in the Consecutive-Sample Model. But the increased
accuracy is obtained at the expense of the RT being longer. It is interesting also to consider what happens in the Consecutive-Sample Model
when the circuit makes a third comparison. This exercise is left for the
reader to carry out.

It was noted earlier in this section that a second source of variability
in the RT of the responses produced by the Comparison-With-Standard
Model is the frequency of the gating signals. RT increases as frequency
of the gating signal decreases in the same way that it does in the case of
the Consecutive-Sample Model. For this reason, Figure 26 is applicable
as well to the Comparison-With-Standard Model. Nevertheless, there is
a difference in the outcome between the two different models. Again,
this difference arises from the fact that the model can take a second look
at the signal environment and make a second comparison. Figure 28
shows how this feature of the model affects the RT when the temporal
location of the stimulus with respect to the gating signals is kept constant, and gating signal frequency is allowed to vary.

Three different values of gating signal frequency are shown in decreasing order in the diagrams of Figure 28. In the example at the bottom, the frequency is only about one-half of the value in the example at
the top. As frequency is the reciprocal of IGI, this decrease in frequency
corresponds to an increase in the IGI. The increments in the duration of
IGI from the upper to the middle and from the middle to the lower diagrams in the figure are equal. As IGI increases, there is an increase in
the RT. For each different value of gating signal frequency, the figure
shows when a response would occur after the circuit has made one and

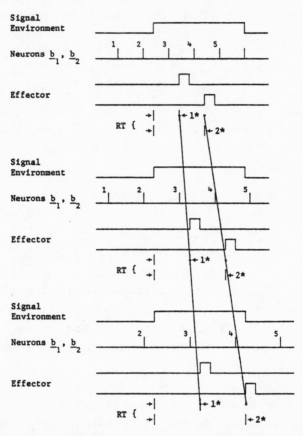

Figure 28: Abbreviated timing diagrams for the Comparison-With-Standard Model of simple RT when frequency of the gating signal is allowed to vary and responses are elicited after 1 and 2 comparisons. The numbers with asterisks refer to the number of comparisons made between a sample of the signal environment and the standard, or sample in storage, before a response is elicited.

then two comparisons of the signal environment with the standard. To show the way in which the RT increases with increasing IGI, a straight line in each case connects the points of response in the diagrams.

Of especial interest in the present context is the slopes of these two straight lines. Note that the slopes are different from each other. The reason for this will become apparent from a close inspection of Figure 28. It will be seen that after one comparison, the range of variation of the RT is equal to the range of variation of the IGI. When the response occurs after two comparisons, the range of variation of the RT increases to *twice* the range of variation of the IGI. If the response had occurred after three comparisons, the range of variation of the RT would have increased to three times this amount, and so on. The lines of different slope indicate, of course, that there is an interaction between the frequency of the gating signals and the number of comparisons made before a response is elicited. The interaction means that, with each additional possible comparison, the RT not only becomes longer but also more variable. In other words, the RTs in the case of the slower-responding examples of the model will tend to be more variable than the RTs of the faster-responding examples.

The Role of Attention

Throughout our discussion in this chapter, it has been assumed that the attention was steadily fixed on the task at hand. From the standpoint of our models and the hypothesis regarding attention that was formulated in Chapter 4, this means that the gating signals were always present in the *b* neurons while the models were functioning. The limitations of such an assumption are obvious. Common knowledge as well as careful research tell us that the attention normally fluctuates from one moment to the next. Let us see what happens to the behavior of our models when the attention is allowed to fluctuate so that the gating signals are not always present in the *b* neurons.

Figure 29 shows how the RT of the Comparison-With-Standard Model varies with changes in the focus of attention. In the diagram at the top of the figure, the attention is focused upon the task prior to the occurrence of the stimulus. This means that gating signals are present in the *b* neurons before the stimulus occurs. As the diagram shows, the gating signals continue to be present until the stimulus is processed and the response is completed. This example, of course, illustrates conditions of stimulation that are identical to those already dealt with in this chapter; it is repeated here only for purposes of comparison with the following examples.

In the diagram at the middle of Figure 29, the stimulus occurs while the attention is turned away from the task. However, after gating signal 3 goes by, the attention focuses in on the task and gating signal 4 is brought to bear on the circuit. Once this happens, the circuit becomes activated and the sample of the signal environment in the interval between gating signals 4 and 5 is compared with the standard stored in memory. The sample and standard are judged to be the same so that a response is elicited after gating signal 5. It will be observed that the RT for this response is one gating cycle longer than it is in the example given at the top of the figure.

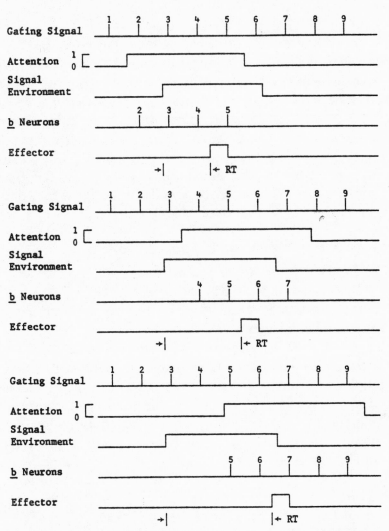

Figure 29: Effect of fluctuations in attention on the RT of responses elicited by the Comparison-With-Standard Model of simple RT.

A similar pattern occurs in the example at the bottom of Figure 29. In this case, gating signals 3 and 4 are missed and the attention becomes focused upon the task only when gating signal 5 comes up. Following the same logic as before, it is clear that no response will occur until gating signal 6 comes along. As a result, the RT will be two gating cycles longer than in the comparison example at the top. We see, therefore, that when the attention is allowed to fluctuate so that the gating signal is sometimes absent from the *b* neurons, the RTs of the responses produced by the model become longer and more variable. Specifically, if the attention is not focused on the task at the time a stimulus occurs, the RT will be prolonged by multiples of the IGI corresponding to the number of gating signals that are missed by the stimulus.

Looking again at Figure 29, it will be seen that the examples shown apply equally as well to the Consecutive-Sample Model. Consider, for example, the case of the diagram at the center of the figure. The stimulus that fills the interval between gating signals 4 and 5 will be fed into input 2 of the comparator circuit. Since nothing yet is in the memory circuit, the comparator will be silent. With no inhibitory input to prevent gating signal 5 from firing neuron *a*, a response will be elicited exactly as shown in the diagram. Fluctuations in attention, therefore, will have a similar effect on the Consecutive-Sample Model that they have on the Comparison-With-Standard Model.

Characteristics of RT in the Proposed Models

We have seen that the major sources of variability in the RT of responses elicited by our models are (1) the temporal location of a stimulus with respect to the gating signals, (2) the frequency of the gating signals, and (3) the number of gating cycles that enter into the response. We found that two factors were responsible for a greater number of gating cycles entering into a response. One factor was associated with the fact that additional comparisons could be made between the signal environment and a standard in order to increase the accuracy of stimulus detection. The other factor was the fluctuation of attention, which from the standpoint of our models means that gating signals are not always present in the *b* neurons. Both factors make the RT longer by adding multiples of the gating cycle to the response. In the course of our discussion, we also observed that there was an interaction between frequency of the gating signals and number of gating cycles in the response. The result of this interaction was that generally slow responses or responses having long RTs were more variable than generally fast responses or those having short RTs.

Let us now examine the characteristics of the RT in the models when the various sources of variability are permitted to change at the same time. We begin with a consideration of the RT within an individual model. This is equivalent to the case in which the RTs of an individual person participating in an experiment are investigated. Later, we will examine the characteristics of the RT in different examples of the same model and consider how these characteristics differ as a function of differences in the sources of variability. The latter is analogous to investigations of RT carried out on different individuals or different groups of individuals.

Characteristics of the RT Within Individual Models

Figure 30 shows the RT plotted against IGI, the reciprocal of gating signal frequency, for conditions in which one, two, or three gating cycles enter into the responses of an individual model. Time on both axes of the graph is in milliseconds. Besides the time consumed in detecting the stimulus and processing the response, there is a delay associated with the fact that it takes time to get information from the receptor to the input of the comparator circuit. In addition, a delay occurs between the time when the *a* neuron signals for a response, and when the effector actually responds. It is assumed that these afferent and efferent delays are constants for a particular model, and amount to a total of about 80 msec.[2]

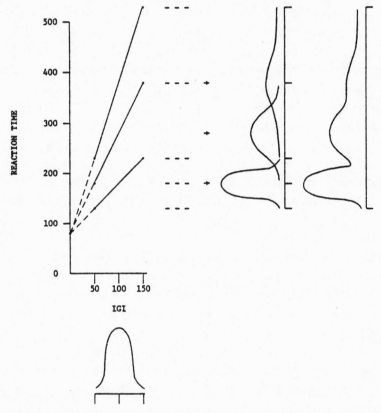

Figure 30: RT vs. IGI and the distribution of RT in the proposed models when one, two, and three gating cycles enter into the response. RT and IGI are in milliseconds. See text for explanation of details.

---

[2]The value of 80 msec is derived from the fact that the latency of P_1, the first major component of the cortical evoked response to an auditory stimulus, ranges between 50-60 msec (Davis, Mast, Yoshie, and Zerlin, 1966; Surwillo, 1977a). This leaves 20-30 msec for the response time of the effector, which would be a minimum value according to available evidence (Surwillo, 1968).

The graph in Figure 30 shows that the IGI varies between 50 and 150 msec. This means that gating signal frequency has a range of 6.7-20 cycles/sec. If — as we hypothesized in Chapter 3 — the EEG is the physiological basis of the gating signal, these values would include levels of consciousness in humans from drowsiness to high-level alertness.[3] We assume that the distribution of IGI is normal with the mean at 100 msec, or 10 cycles/sec, which is the mean frequency of the alpha rhythm in adults.

A further assumption in Figure 30 is that the phase of the gating cycle in which the stimuli fall is constant from trial to trial. By making such an assumption, the increases in RT that take place with increases in the IGI can be represented by straight lines. For example, with one gating cycle entering into the responses, the RT is $80 + 50 = 130$ msec for $IGI = 50$ msec, and $80 + 150 = 230$ msec for $IGI = 150$ msec. When two gating cycles enter into the responses, the RT is $80 + 2 \times 50 = 180$ msec for $IGI = 50$ msec, and $80 + 2 \times 150 = 380$ msec for $IGI = 150$ msec. These, of course, are both linear relationships. A similar relationship holds true for the case involving three gating cycles. The graphs describe the relationship between RT and IGI for the Comparison-With-Standard Model as well as the Consecutive-Sample Model. In the case of the former model, the different number of gating cycles entering into a response are due to trial-to-trial fluctuations in attention, to additional comparisons being made between the signal environment and the standard, or to a combination of both. In the case of the Consecutive-Sample Model, the differences are due primarily to trial-to-trial fluctuations in attention.

Under these conditions it is apparent that values of RT and IGI will be positively correlated. But the correlation could vary considerably from one individual model to another, and in general will not be very high. This happens for a number of reasons. The correlations are subject to fluctuation resulting from sampling. They will be reduced by the fact that the relationship between RT and IGI for the three conditions combined is not linear but funnel-shaped. Note in Figure 30, that as the number of gating cycles entering into the responses increases, the

---

[3]The waking electrical rhythm of the brain — the so-called alpha rhythm — normally includes frequencies in the range of 8-13 cycles/sec. During drowsiness and the early stages of sleep, the alpha rhythm gives way to the theta rhythm, which consists of frequencies having a range of 4-8 cycles/sec. Frequencies greater than 13 cycles/sec — referred to as the beta rhythm — may occur when a person is very alert or excited. If we assumed that the gating signal included frequencies only in the alpha range, IGI would vary between 77 and 125 msec.

width of this funnel also increases; and with this increase comes a decrease in the correlation. Conversely, a decrease in the number of cycles entering into the responses will be accompanied by a larger correlation.

The magnitude of the correlation between RT and IGI will further be reduced if the phase of the gating cycle in which the stimuli fall is free to vary as in the case of an actual RT experiment. Thus, if a stimulus occurs at such a time that an upcoming gating cycle is missed, processing would be delayed until the next gating signal came along. The net result is that the RT would be prolonged. If this happened a sufficient number of times when the IGI was a minimum value, it is easy to see that the correlation between RT and IGI could become zero—or even slightly negative—if the distribution of IGI were restricted in range.

The separate distributions of RT produced by one, two, and three gating cycles entering into the responses are shown at the right in Figure 30. RT in milliseconds and frequency of occurrence of different values of RT appear, respectively, on the vertical and horizontal coordinates. Note that, as each additional gating cycle is added, the range of the RT distributions becomes correspondingly larger. At the far right of the figure is the distribution of RT obtained by summing together the three separate distributions on the left. A combined distribution like this would normally be obtained in a RT experiment unless some way of sorting the responses into separate distributions were available.

The distributions of the RT in our models, thus, have three distinguishing characteristics. In the first place, they are skewed in the positive direction. Secondly, they are multi-modal—i.e., the distributions have more than one peak. Thirdly, these peaks are separated by intervals equal to the mean of the distribution of the IGI. This interval is 100 msec in the case of Figure 30, where the peaks of the separate distributions are indicated by the short arrows. A careful study of the diagram reveals that the peaks in the composite distribution will become more clearly defined as the range of the IGI decreases and there is less overlap in the components of the distribution. On the other hand, the peaks will tend to be obscured as the range of the IGI increases. If the phase of the gating cycle in which the stimuli fall is free to vary, the peaks will further be obscured, but in this case by the added variability of the distribution.

These, then, are the major characteristics of the RT as displayed by our model. Now let us turn from our model and the features it displays to a consideration of the characteristics of the RT of human subjects.

The Human RT—Characteristics and Psychophysiology Within Individuals

Distributions of the RT in individual human subjects are usually found to be positively skewed. The reason generally given is that the distribution is free to vary in the direction of longer RTs, but that physiological limits within the organism restrict variation in the other direction. While this explanation is plausible, the precise mechanisms involved have not been spelled out. On the other hand, the models proposed in the present work provide a simple mechanism whereby such positively skewed distributions may be generated. Our discussion in the previous section of this chapter shows how the distributions actually come about.

A number of investigators have found multiple peaks in the distributions of RTs from single subjects (Harter and White, 1968; Latour, 1967; Pöppel, 1970; Venables, 1960). The time between consecutive peaks in such distributions was reported to range between 25-100 msec. In a hypothesis that foreshadows the present work, Venables (1960) suggested that the long RTs in such distributions indicate that a cycle of excitation has, in some way, been missed. Venables's cycle of excitation bears a close resemblance to the gating cycle as proposed in our models of simple RT.

An experiment carried out by the author (Surwillo, 1975) investigated the RT in individual subjects under conditions that were expected to increase the likelihood that different numbers of gating cycles would enter into a response and hence facilitate the occurrence of multiple peaks in the distribution of RT. Two different conditions were employed in a reaction task that used a 1000 Hz tone as the stimulus. In one condition, the tones were presented at an intensity level of 74 dB; these tones followed one another closely in time, with the interval between successive presentations varying at random between 6 and 8 sec. This condition was expected to yield short RTs having a narrow range of variation. In the other condition, the tones were presented at only 44 dB. Since the tones were heard against an ambient noise level of 33dB, the subject had to listen very carefully so as not to miss them. The intervals between successive tones in this case were much longer and more variable; they had a range of 6-40 sec, and varied at random in steps of 1 sec. Thus, there were times when the subject had to wait a long time indeed before the next stimulus came along. This condition was expected to favor long, highly variable RTs.

Figure 31 shows the outcome of this experiment in two of the subjects tested. The solid lines are distributions of RT for the condition expected to yield short RTs of low variability and the dashed lines are for the condition expected to favor long, highly variable RTs. The distributions in each case were based upon a total of 140 trials. It is readily apparent from an inspection of these curves that the results confirmed the expectations. The means of the solid-line distributions are substantially smaller than the means of the dashed-line distributions. In addition, the dashed-line distributions show considerably more variability in the RT than the solid-line distributions.

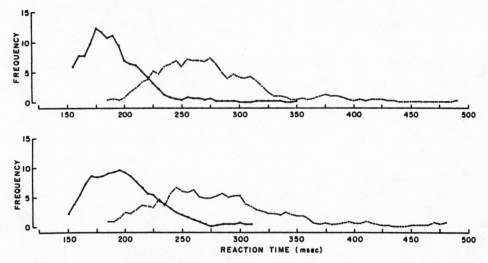

Figure 31: Distributions of the RT in a 24 year-old male (above) and a 26 year-old male (below) obtained under conditions favoring short RTs of low variability (solid lines) and long, highly-variable RTs (dashed lines). Taken from Figure 2 of Surwillo, W.W.: *Biological Psychology*, 1975, *3*, 247-261, by courtesy of North-Holland Publishing Company, Amsterdam.

The curves of human RT seen in Figure 31 look remarkably like the RT distributions in Figure 30 that were generated by the models proposed in Chapter 5. The graph in the upper half of Figure 31 appears to have three peaks and closely resembles the composite distribution of RT shown in Figure 30 for the proposed models. The graph in the lower half of Figure 31 has two peaks; it looks like the RT distribution produced by the models when, at times, one gating cycle and, at other times, two gating cycles enter into the responses. Although the peaks of the distributions cannot be located precisely, those in the graph at the top of Figure 31 appear to occur at about 175, 265, and 375 msec, while those at the bottom are at approximately 190 and 265 msec. This means that the time between consecutive peaks in these distributions ranged between 75 and 110 msec. EEGs were also obtained for these subjects and the means of the EEG distributions were found to fall well within these limits (Surwillo, 1975).

But what about the relationship between the RT and the frequency of the gating signal? If the EEG is the physiological basis of the gating signal as was hypothesized in Chapter 3, then the RT and EEG should be related, with faster frequencies in the EEG going along with shorter RTs and vice versa. To answer this question, the EEG was recorded at the same time that the reaction task was being performed. Using the tracing obtained from electrodes placed over the parietal-occipital area on the left side of the scalp,[4] we estimated the average duration of the waves — the EEG period — in the interval between stimulus and response for each trial. The measurements upon which these estimates were based were carried out manually, using a set of strict rules that had been developed earlier (Surwillo, 1963a, 1971). The Pearson product-moment coefficient of correlation between RT and EEG period proved to be positive and, thus, in accord with the hypothesis; but the value of +0.62 was not remarkable for its size. A scatter plot of these data, which appears in Figure 32, shows why.

Figure 32 makes it clear that the points defining the relationship between RT and EEG period in this individual would be only poorly represented by a single, best-fitting straight line. Rather than forming an ellipse as often is the case in a linear regression, the distribution of points is funnel-shaped. But this distribution takes on meaning when the straight lines defining the relationship between RT and IGI in our models of simple RT are drawn on the graph. These lines come from Figure 30. The upper line, it will be noted, shows how RT increases with increasingly longer IGIs when two gating cycles enter into the responses; the lower line describes the same relationship for only one gating cycle. Note how the points tend to cluster about the two lines, suggesting that the model may indeed be defining what is going on in the human subject. With the addition of these lines, therefore, a possible mechanism that could account for this otherwise confusing variability is brought to light. Naturally, further research along these lines will be needed in order to test the ultimate strength of the model.

---

[4]The parietal-occipital derivation was used because this recording site usually furnished the greatest amounts of alpha rhythm activity.

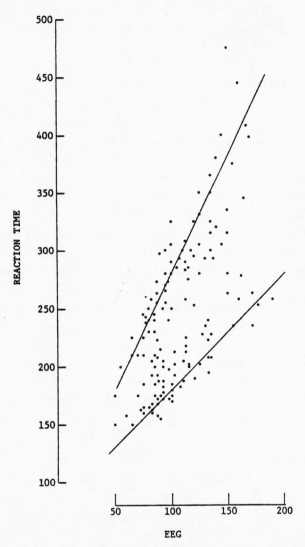

Figure 32: Reaction time in milliseconds vs. the EEG, or average duration in milliseconds of waves recorded in the interval between stimulus and response. EEGs from the parietal-occipital derivation on the left. Data from a 26 year-old male.

In another study (Surwillo, 1963a), the relationship between RT and EEG period was investigated in 99 human subjects. The subjects took part in a simple RT experiment in which they were asked to press a button as quickly as possible whenever a 250 Hz tone, that was well above the threshold, was presented over a loudspeaker. The tones, which occurred at random, lasted for approximately 3 sec; no forewarning or "ready" signal was given prior to their presentation. The task was performed while the subjects rested comfortably with the eyes closed, in a darkened room. A total of 90 stimuli were presented in three separate sessions. The first and second sessions were identical; but part way through the third session, the duration of the tones changed abruptly from 3 to 0.3 sec. Subjects were told about this change beforehand. They were asked to pay especially close attention to the stimuli when this change occurred, and to concentrate the greatest possible effort on responding quickly. In this way we hoped to obtain some of their shortest RTs. Because the subjects frequently became drowsy in the first two sessions, the experiment provided data over a wide range of conditions, from drowsiness to high-level alertness.

As in the previously-described experiment, an estimate of the period of the EEG in the interval between stimulus and response was obtained for each trial. These data were used to compute a Pearson product-moment coefficient of correlation between RT and EEG period for each of the 99 subjects. The solid line in Figure 33 is the frequency distribution of these coefficients after the correlations had been transformed into Fisher z's. Fisher z's were obtained so that the coefficients could be averaged and a mean computed for the distribution of 99 coefficients. Ninety-three of the 99 coefficients proved to be positive and average z was 0.312, which corresponds to a Pearson coefficient of 0.302. Since standard error of the mean was only 0.02, the mean of 0.312 was clearly not attributable to chance factors operating through sampling.

Evidence cited from the experiment just discussed leaves little doubt that there is a relationship between RT and EEG period within individual subjects, with long RTs being associated with long-duration waves (low frequencies) in the EEG and vice versa. The relatively low value of the correlation coefficients defining this relationship was predicted from our model of simple RT. The factors responsible for the low correlations were discussed in the last section. At that time, it was shown that the correlation between RT and IGI in the models would vary according to the number of gating cycles entering into the responses, with larger correlations going along with the presence of fewer gating cycles. Such being the case, we should expect that the correlations between RT and EEG period in individual subjects would be increased by raising the overall level of attention and thus limiting the number of gating cycles that enter into the response. In the context of the experiment under discussion, we would predict that the correlations obtained when the subjects were asked to pay particularly close attention to the task would be larger than the correlations obtained using data from the experiment as a whole.

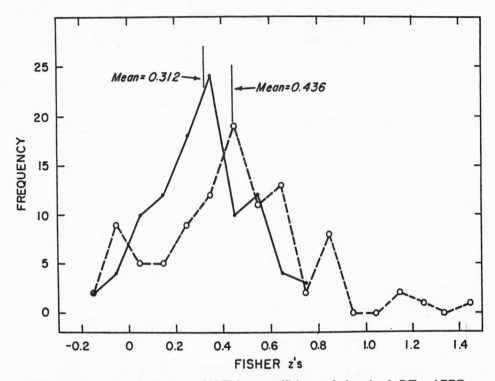

Figure 33: Frequency distributions of 99 Fisher z coefficients relating simple RT and EEG period within individuals. The solid line shows the distribution of coefficients obtained under conditions where the attention was expected to vary over a wide range; the dashed line shows the distribution of coefficients obtained when special efforts were made to keep the attention focused on the task. Reprint of Figure 4 from Surwillo, W.W.: *Electroencephalography and Clinical Neurophysiology,* 1963a, *15,* 105-114, by permission of Elsevier Biomedical Press, Amsterdam.

This expectation was fulfilled by the data. The dashed line in Figure 33 is the distribution of Fisher z's derived from data obtained when the subjects were maintaining high levels of attention. Note that the entire distribution of z's is shifted to the right. The mean of this distribution is 0.436, which corresponds to a Pearson coefficient of 0.410.

Figure 34 shows what some of the actual data collected in the experiment looked like. Here we find four of the 90 trials that were recorded in one of the 99 subjects. The figure includes the shortest (255 msec) and the longest RT (640 msec) produced by this subject, as well as two trials in which the RTs were of intermediate length. Note how the frequency of the EEG differs in the four trials. When the RT was only 255 msec long, frequency of the EEG in the interval between stimulus and response was about 10 cycles/sec. At the opposite extreme, EEG frequency dropped to about 6 cycles/sec when the RT was 640 msec.

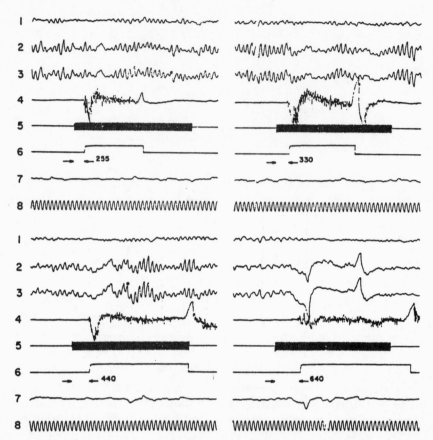

Figure 34: EEGs recorded during performance of a simple RT task. Channels 1, 2, and 3 are EEGs from transverse occipital, left occipital, and right occipital derivations, respectively; channel 4, electromyogram from flexor brevis pollicis; channel 5, stimulus marker; channel 6, response marker; channel 7, transverse frontal leads (for monitoring eye-movement artifacts); channel 8, calibration signal, 60μV, 10 c/sec. Numbers beside channel 6 are the RTs in msec. Figure 5 from Surwillo, W.W.: *Electroencephalography and Clinical Neurophysiology,* 1963a, *15,* 105-114; reprinted by permission of Elsevier Biomedical Press, Amsterdam.

As far as the RT within individuals is concerned, therefore, the models of simple RT proposed in Chapter 5 seem to fit the available evidence rather well. The models appear to be able to account for the phenomenon of RT variability. In addition, they provide a plausible mechanism for explaining some of the major characteristics of the RT in individuals. Evidence from the psychophysiology of simple RT within individuals appears to be in accord with the concept of central timing. These data suggest that the frequency of the EEG has all the requisite characteristics of a gating signal — the proposed mechanism that was found to play such a major role in the functioning of the proposed models.

Data concerning the RT in relation to the phase of the EEG are scarce. For this reason, the effects of this factor on the human RT are difficult to evaluate. Callaway (1962) and Callaway and Yeager (1960) have reported that simple RT is a function of the particular phase of the EEG wave in which a stimulus falls. In a related experiment, Nunn and Osselton (1974) found that there was a relationship between the perception of a stimulus and the phase of the alpha rhythm in which the stimulus was presented. Thus, a stimulus was perceived when it happened to occur at some alpha phases, but was not perceived when it occurred at others. But details of these relationships are lacking. About all we presently can say about the matter is that the evidence is not in disagreement with the proposed models.

Characteristics of the RT Between Individual Models

In this section, we consider the RT in different versions of the same model. We will examine the way in which the RT in these models may differ in relation to differences in the values of their parameters.

Let us consider what happens when two versions of the same model, models A and B, are alike in every respect except that the frequency of the gating signal is higher in A than it is in B. From our previous discussions, it is obvious that the RT in the two models will differ, with model B having longer RTs than model A. But what will happen if, at the same time, the number of gating cycles entering into the responses is free to vary in both models? Figure 35 addresses this question when one and two gating cycles enter into the responses.

As seen in Figure 35, the IGI in the two models is normally distributed. IGI has a range of 40 msec in both distributions, but the mean of the distribution in model A is 90 msec, while the comparable value in model B is 110 msec. The distributions of the RT for the two models are shown in the figure at the right. Note that, with only one gating cycle entering into the responses, the distributions of RT are identical to the distribution of IGI, except that the mean of the distribution in model B is 20 msec longer than the mean of the distribution in model A. When two gating cycles enter into the responses, however, the range of the RT distributions is doubled, and the mean of the B distribution is 40 msec longer than the mean of the A distribution. In other words, adding an additional gating cycle to the RT makes the RT longer and twice as variable.

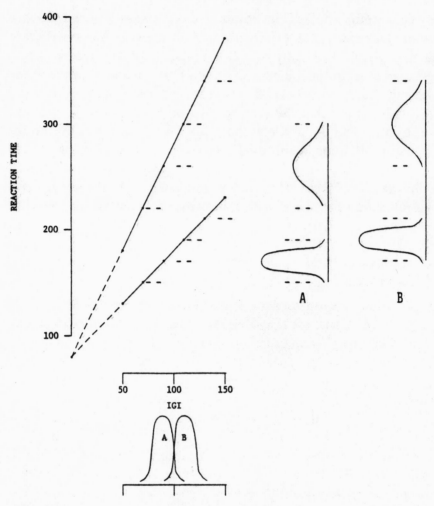

Figure 35: RT vs. IGI and the distributions of the RT in models A and B when one and two gating cycles enter into the responses. RT and IGI are in milliseconds. Models A and B are identical with the exception that the mean of the distribution of IGIs is larger by 20 msec in B than in A.

What happens when the RT distributions for one and two gating cycles are combined, however, is the matter of present concern. At the outset, it should be recognized that our example in Figure 35 assumes that the phase of the gating cycles in which the stimuli fall is constant. With the added variability that results from allowing the phase of the gating cycle to vary, the two components of the distributions will be less discrete. Nevertheless, the combined RT distributions will show that average RT is longer in model B than in model A. Of especial interest, however, is the fact that the difference between the RTs in the two models is larger than the difference between their mean IGIs. This singular feature of the model comes about because of the interaction between frequency of the gating signal and the number of gating cycles. The interaction is important because it means that — although IGI is a determinant of the RT — the magnitude of any difference in the IGI between two versions of the same model may not be sufficient to account for the resulting difference observed in the RT. So an important characteristic of our model is that the distributions of RTs from individuals having generally slow responses will show greater variability than the distributions from individuals having generally fast responses.

The Human RT — Characteristics and Psychophysiology Between Individuals

If our models of simple RT are to be of any value insofar as understanding the variability in the RT between different individuals is concerned, certain expectations must be met. In the first place, we should expect individuals or groups of individuals having long RTs to have EEGs that are composed of lower frequencies than individuals having short RTs. Secondly, we should expect persons having long RTs to have RTs that are also more variable and vice versa. In other words, longer RTs should go together with more variable RTs, and shorter RTs with less variable RTs. Finally, we expect that, in the main, the magnitude of any difference in RT between two individuals will be greater than the corresponding EEG difference between these same individuals. How much greater will depend upon the number of gating cycles entering into the responses. This means, of course, that the extent of the role played by the EEG in determining the RT cannot be defined simply by comparing the difference in the EEG period between two individuals with the difference in their RTs. Fortunately, these propositions are easily tested because the RT shows major differences between large groups of individuals.

It is well-known that the RT is longer in children than in young adults (see, e.g., Hohle, 1967), and that RT becomes longer again in old age (Welford, 1959). These differences served as the vehicle for testing our predictions from the models of simple RT. Table I shows the major findings in investigations of simple RT and EEG period in adults aged 28-99 years, and in children 4-17 years. As in the previously-described investigations, EEGs were recorded from the parietal-occipital derivation while the subjects performed a reaction task. Pure tones served as the stimuli; they were presented at levels well above the threshold, were widely spaced in time, and occurred at random without any warning signal. The average duration of waves recorded in the interval between stimulus and response was reckoned for each trial, and the mean of these values was computed for each subject. Similarly, a mean value of the RT was obtained for each subject.

TABLE I

RT AND EEG DATA FROM SEPARATE EXPERIMENTS IN WHICH
CHILDREN AND ADULTS, FROM MATURITY THROUGH
OLD AGE, SERVED AS SUBJECTS

	Children[1] (4-17 years)	Adults[2] (28-99 years)
RT (msec):		
Mean	324	259
Mean σ_{RT}	53	29
Range	200-800	190-350
EEG Period (msec):		
Mean	112	104
σ	10	39
Range	88-138	84-144
Correlations:		
RT vs. Age	-.87	.19
σ_{RT} vs. Age	-.76	.26
EEG Period vs. Age	-.50	.57
RT vs. EEG Period	.50	.72
N	110	100

[1]Data from Surwillo (1971).
[2]Data from Surwillo (1963a, b).

Looking at Table I, we see that the experiments confirm the expectations in every respect. Note, first, that the correlation between RT and age is negative in children during the developmental years and positive in adults who range in age from maturity through old age. In other words, the RT of young children is longer than the RT of older children, and old adults have longer RTs than young adults. Along with these differences is the finding of a positive correlation between RT and EEG period in both groups— +0.50 in children and +0.72 in adults. These data, of course, confirm our first expectation.

Moving on to the matter of variability in the RT, we find in Table I that σ_{RT}—the standard deviation of the RT in each subject—is correlated with age in the same way as the RT. This is true both in the children and the adults. Just as the younger children's RTs are longer than the older children's RTs, so the variability of the RT is greater in the younger than the older children. Similarly, the RTs of the old adults are more variable as well as being longer than the RTs of the young adults. The same characteristics are displayed by the means of the two groups. Thus, the mean RT is 324–259 = 65 msec longer in the group of 110 children than in the group of 100 adults. Corresponding to this difference, the mean of the standard deviations of RT in the group of children is 24 msec longer, or nearly twice the value it is in the adults. In short, the data make it clear that long RTs are more variable than short RTs.

Turning now to the EEG data themselves, Table I shows that EEG period and age are correlated in both groups. The correlation of –0.50 in children means that frequency of the EEG increases with age during the developmental years. At the other end of the life-span, the correlation of +0.57 in adults indicates that frequency of the EEG decreases in old age. The RT and EEG data for the children have been plotted in Figure 36. The same data for the adults appear in Figure 37. In each case, the best-fitting straight line derived from the correlational analysis has been drawn on the figure. Note that both graphs have some of the funnel-shaped characteristics mentioned in our earlier discussion of IGI and EEG within individuals. In both instances, it is apparent that the range of variation of the RT exceeds the range of the EEG. As Table I shows, the range of the RT is between 2 and 3 times greater than the range of the EEG period in adults, and 12 times greater in children.

In summary then, evidence from the psychophysiology of simple RT between individuals appears to be in accord with the proposed models of simple RT. EEG frequency appears to play a major role in the RT of human subjects in the same way that gating signal frequency does in the RT of the models. It is impossible, of course, to argue from these data

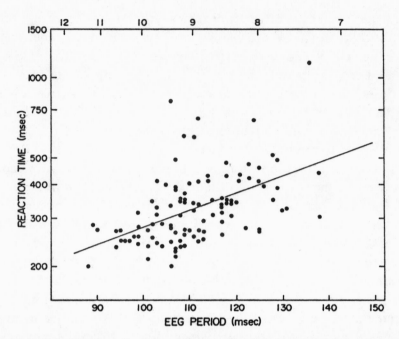

Figure 36: Relationship between RT and EEG period in healthy children, aged 4-17 years (N = 110). Copyright© 1971, The Society for Psychophysiological Research. Reprinted with permission of the publisher from Surwillo, W.W.: Human reaction time and period of the EEG in relation to development. *Psychophysiology,* 1971, *8*, 468-482, Figure 4.

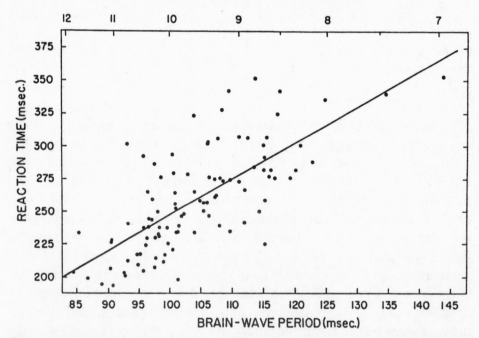

Figure 37: Relationship between RT and EEG period in healthy adults, aged 28-99 years (N = 100). Numbers at the top of the graph refer to the corresponding values of frequency in cycles per second. Reprint of Figure 2 from Surwillo, W.W.: *Electroencephalography and Clinical Neurophysiology,* 1963a, *15*, 105-114, by permission of Elsevier Biomedical Press, Amsterdam.

that the EEG itself is the causal factor in behavioral slowing. Nevertheless, this evidence does suggest that frequency of the EEG may be a determining factor in the longer RT that characterizes the responses of children and old people. What happens when the frequency of the EEG is altered experimentally is considered in the next section.

The Experimental Alteration of EEG Frequency

As mentioned briefly in Chapter 3, an interesting characteristic displayed by the EEG is the phenomenon of photic "driving." In photic driving, brief flashes of intense light are presented to the subject at repetition rates that are within the normal frequency range of the EEG. The flashes are presented in such a way that they cover the entire visual field, producing a so-called "ganzfeld." When this happens, the spontaneous electrical activity of the brain appears to become synchronized with the flashes of light; if, then, the repetition rate of the flashes is varied, the frequency of the EEG appears to follow this variation. Figure 38 illustrates the phenomenon in a subject whose EEGs could be "driven" over the range of 7.6-12.5 cycles/sec. Aside from the fact that the frequency of the waves during actual driving is constant, the tracings look no different from EEGs that are recorded under normal resting conditions.

The actual mechanism whereby this phenomenon is produced is unknown. In Chapter 3, we hypothesized that the EEG as observed on the scalp is the electrical manifestation of the secretion, at large numbers of synapses in the cortex, of neural transmitter produced by the activity of the thalamic pacemaker neurons. If this hypothesis were indeed correct, then one possible explanation of the phenomenon of photic driving is that the flashing light is mimicking the effects of the pacemaker neurons and taking over control of cortical synchronization from them. From the standpoint of our models of simple RT, this would mean that the repetition rate of the flashing light could determine the frequency of the cortical gating cycle. If this were to happen, the phenomenon could have a far-reaching effect on the RT.

To test out this idea, the author had subjects perform a reaction task at the same time that the frequency of the EEG was being controlled by means of photic driving (Surwillo, 1964a). Photic driving over the range of 6-15 flashes per second was attempted in a total of 48 adult subjects. Of those tested, all but five showed no evidence of synchronization with the flashing light or manifested synchronization over only a very narrow range of flash rates while taking part in the experiment. The EEGs in

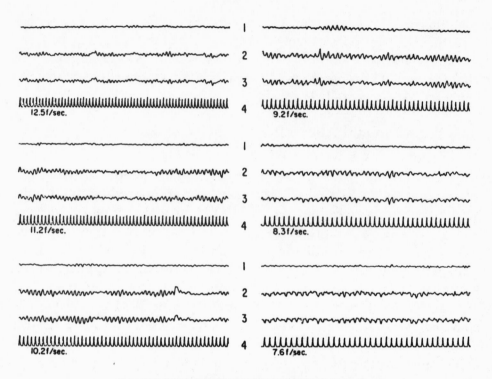

Figure 38: EEGs recorded during photic "driving" at various repetition rates. Channel 1, 2, and 3 are EEGs from transverse occipital, left occipital, and right occipital derivations, respectively; channel 4, photic driving signal. Numbers at the lower left-hand corner of each set of tracings refer to the frequency of the flashes. Figure 1 from Surwillo, W.W.: *Electroencephalography and Clinical Neurophysiology*, 1964a, *17*, 194-198; reprinted by permission of Elsevier Biomedical Press, Amsterdam.

the remaining five subjects could be synchronized over flash rates that covered an average range of 4 flashes per second. Figure 39 shows three of the trials from one of these five subjects. Note that the RTs are shorter when the flash rates are higher and vice versa.

For each of the five subjects who displayed noticeable EEG synchronization, a Pearson product-moment correlation coefficient was computed between RT and period of the driving signal. The coefficients, which were all positive, were equal to 0.10, 0.52, 0.55, 0.49, and 0.32. An overall test of significance showed that the probability of the combination of these five correlations occurring by chance was less than 0.001. Similar correlation coefficients were computed for a control group composed of five subjects whose EEGs showed no synchronization with the flashing light while participating in the RT experiment. In this case, the coefficients were negative as well as positive and clustered around zero.

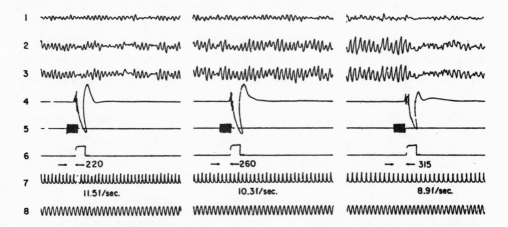

Figure 39: Three trials of a simple RT task performed during photic "driving" at various repetition rates. Channels 1, 2, and 3 are EEGs from transverse occipital, left occipital, and right occipital derivations, respectively; channel 4 electromyogram from flexor brevis pollicis; channel 5, stimulus marker; channel 6, response marker; channel 7, photic driving signal; channel 8, 60μV, 10 c/sec calibration. Numbers below channel 6 are the RTs in msec. Figure 2 from Surwillo, W.W.: *Electroencephalography and Clinical Neurophysiology,* 1964a, *17,* 194-198; reprinted by permission of Elsevier Biomedical Press, Amsterdam.

This experiment has been replicated in another laboratory with the same result. Thus, Waszak (1965) found coefficients of $+0.271$ (N=48) and $+0.542$ (N=67) between RT and period of the photic driving signal in two subjects that were tested in the laboratory at Duke University. The findings of these photic driving experiments are in accord with our concept of central timing. They suggest that a person's RT may actually be manipulated by changing the frequency of his or her EEGs.

Another study in which the frequency of the EEG was manipulated experimentally during performance of a simple RT task has been reported by Woodruff (1975). In this remarkable investigation, the technique of biofeedback was employed to modify EEG frequency in 10 young and 10 old adults. Subjects were trained to increase the amount of time during which they showed frequencies in their EEGs that were 2 Hz faster and 2 Hz slower than their modal frequency. Immediately after a set criterion of success was achieved — and while the biofeedback task continued — the subjects performed a simple RT task in which clicks of moderate intensity were the stimuli. The clicks were presented at random intervals of approximately 2-5 sec.

The results of Woodruff's study indicated that experimental alteration of EEG frequency affected the RT. When the subjects produced fast waves in their EEGs, the RT was significantly shorter than when they produced slow waves. Details of the relationship are shown in Figure 40. Here we see that, in the young subjects, there was a difference of 12 msec in the period of the EEG between the slow-wave and fast-wave feedback conditions. This was accompanied by a difference in the RT of 22 msec in the expected direction. In the old subjects, the comparable EEG difference was 14 msec, and this difference was accompanied by a difference of 36 msec in the RT. Woodruff's findings, therefore, appear to be in agreement with the results obtained using photic driving to alter EEG frequency; moreover, they are in accord with the proposed models and with the concept of central timing.

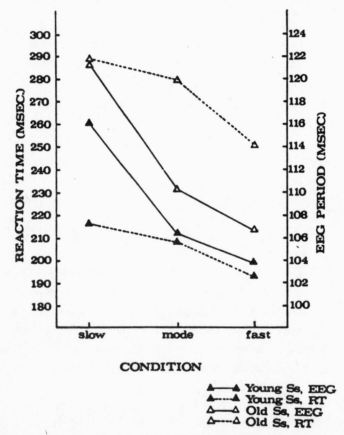

Figure 40: RT and period of the EEG in young and old subjects under baseline conditions and during biofeedback designed to decrease and increase EEG frequency. Slow and fast on the horizontal axis correspond to conditions in which biofeedback was used to decrease and increase EEG frequency, respectively. The mode condition is the baseline condition without biofeedback. Copyright© 1975, The Society for Psychophysiological Research. Reprinted with permission of the author and publisher from Woodruff, D.S.: Relationships among EEG alpha frequency, reaction time, and age: A biofeedback study. *Psychophysiology,* 1975, *12,* 673-681, Figure 3.

Other Lines of Evidence

There are a number of other investigations reported in the literature in which the RT and EEG frequency have been found to vary concomitantly. These investigations cover a number of diverse topics and sources. Each of them adds to the store of evidence which suggests that EEG frequency may play a central role in the timing of simple behavior. Some of the more important studies will be mentioned briefly.

It has been suggested that the longer RT and lower frequency EEGs that occur in old age may be due to the effect of lowered cerebral oxygen levels. Thus, for example, Obrist (1964) and Obrist, Sokoloff, Lassen, Lane, Butler, and Feinberg (1963) have presented evidence suggesting that one of the important factors underlying the slow EEGs of old age is a reduction in cerebral oxygen uptake. This evidence is of particular interest when viewed in the context of the studies of McFarland (1932, 1937), who reported that hypoxia produced by ascents to high altitudes resulted in longer RTs. It is not presently known whether cerebral hypoxia has any direct effect on the RT or whether the observed effects are mediated via the slowing in the EEG. The latter would appear to be the more likely possibility in view of the evidence presented earlier. A definitive answer to this question, however, waits on the availability of fresh data.

Acute exposure to carbon dioxide has been shown to have an effect on both the frequency of the EEG and the RT. Harter (1967) investigated the simple RT in five human subjects while they inhaled different concentrations of carbon dioxide ranging from 0-7.9%. Variance analyses of the findings indicated that the percentage of carbon dioxide inhaled significantly affected both the frequency of the EEG and the RT. In particular, the RT was shorter and EEG frequency higher during conditions when 0-5.5% carbon dioxide was administered than when 7.9% carbon dioxide was breathed. The findings within individuals showed a related effect. Thus, within-subject changes in the RT and in EEG frequency across the different carbon dioxide concentrations investigated were negatively correlated.

In an unusual study, Volavka, Levine, Feldstein, and Fink (1974) investigated the effects of heroin on the RT in an auditory detection task and EEG in 19 detoxified addicts. This experiment was prompted by some earlier reports which suggested that heroin produces changes in the EEG that are similar to those usually seen in normal sleep, but yet the subjects seemed behaviorally alert in the presence of the sleep-like

EEG. To investigate this possible dissociation of brain and behavioral events, Volavka and his colleagues recorded the EEG and RT during administration of heroin to find out whether heroin affects the EEG independently of any effects on the RT.

The results of this experiment were definitive. Within 30 minutes of the administration of the drug, average frequency of the EEG decreased from 10.5-8.5 cycles/sec. Corresponding to this change, the RT increased significantly — nearly doubling in length. Administration of a placebo in a control experiment showed no evidence of EEG or RT changes. When the effects of the EEG frequency were accounted for statistically, the relationship between the RT and heroin disappeared. The authors concluded that there was no dissociation between brain and behavioral events, and suggested that the effect of heroin on the RT may be mediated by a mechanism that involves slowing of the EEG frequency. This is in accord with Engel and Romano's (1959) earlier observations that the decrements in behavior and level of consciousness that appear in various stages of delirium are closely correlated with slowing in the EEG.

Another way of slowing down the frequency of the EEG involves the use of hyperventilation.[5] During hyperventilation, the EEGs of some persons show evidences of generalized slow activity. Thus, although the person hyperventilating appears to be awake, frequency of the EEG may drop into the theta range (4 to less than 8 Hz) or sometimes even into the delta range (less than 4 Hz). To discover whether such slowed cerebral electrical activity is associated with a lowered state of awareness, Griesel (1966) recorded the EEG and simple visual RT in normal young men while they were hyperventilating. A group of 23 subjects whose EEGs showed considerable slowing during 3 min of hyperventilation was compared with a control group of 23 subjects having the same mean age but whose EEGs showed no change or only minimal slowing. Mean RT for the control group was 289 msec; for the group showing considerable EEG slowing during hyperventilation, the mean RT was 340 msec. The difference of 51 msec between these values is not only statistically significant (.001 level of confidence) but is also of substantial magnitude.

---

[5]Hyperventilation, or overbreathing, is a standard clinical procedure for activating the EEG. It consists of three minutes of deep breathing through the mouth at a rate of about one inspiration every one or two seconds. This maneuver produces a hypocapnic vasoconstriction of the cerebral blood vessels and results in a reduction in the supply of oxygen to the neurons of the brain.

Griesel (1966) analyzed his data in yet another way. In each of the 23 subjects whose EEGs showed considerable slowing during hyperventilation, the trials having the longest and the shortest RTs were identified. Thereupon, the measurements of EEG frequency obtained during each of these two trials were tabulated and group means were computed. Average EEG frequency was 6.89 Hz for the shortest RTs and 5.64 Hz for the longest RTs. The difference of 1.25 Hz between the two conditions was statistically significant at the .001 level of confidence. So here, again, there is evidence of an association between RT and EEG frequency, with faster frequencies going along with shorter RTs and vice versa.

A related finding has been reported in a study in which an RT task was performed while the 3/sec spike-wave paroxysms associated with absencé attacks were present. Using RT scores obtained before the paroxysms as a control, Browne, Penry, Porter, and Dreifuss (1974) reported that responses obtained following the initiation of paroxysms had RTs that were substantially prolonged. Indeed, whenever the paroxysms happened to be completely generalized, less than 10% of the RTs to an auditory stimulus presented ½ second after the start of the paroxysm were within normal limits. These authors considered as normal all RTs that fell below the 95th percentile of the distribution of RTs obtained when no abnormality was present in the EEG. As the median at the 95th percentile was 670 msec, the vast majority of the responses obtained during spike-wave paroxysms was very markedly delayed indeed. Although these findings are hardly evidence of a causal relationship between simple RT and EEG frequency, they are commensurate with the idea of an association between the two phenomena.

A similar investigation was carried out by Hughes and Cayaffa (1973) using subjects whose EEGs showed evidence of "psychomotor variant" discharges. The psychomotor variant discharge is an intermittently occurring burst of rhythmic, high amplitude 6 Hz waves that have some 12 Hz activity of much lower amplitude mixed in; this faster activity gives the slow waves a notched appearance. These unusual discharges often are found in persons having symptoms resembling those of psychomotor epileptics, but whose attacks usually lack any motor manifestations. Hughes and Cayaffa found that when psychomotor variant discharges were present, some persons did not respond at all in a simple reaction task while others had RTs that were significantly longer than those obtained when the discharges were absent and a normal waking EEG was recorded. In some instances the difference was quite marked, amounting to several hundred milliseconds. As was the case in the other studies we have been discussing, we again have evidence of longer RTs going along with slower frequencies in the EEG.

In a topic far removed from the ones previously considered, Creutzfeldt, Arnold, Becker, Langenstein, Tirsch, Wilhelm, and Wuttke (1976) investigated the EEG and a variety of psychometric tests including the RT in 16 women during a spontaneous menstrual cycle. The EEG findings in the majority of subjects showed functional changes dependent upon the menstrual cycle. These changes consisted of a statistically significant acceleration of 0.3 cycles/sec in the mean frequency of the alpha rhythm during the luteal phase. This increase in EEG frequency was paralleled by an improvement in performance of the psychometric tasks—specifically, a decrease in the RT. The relationship uncovered was far from trivial. Thus, a correlation coefficient of −0.702 was reported between the RT and EEG frequency in the group of 16 subjects.

The foregoing evidence, together with the evidence considered earlier in this chapter, makes it clear that frequency of the EEG is a factor that needs to be reckoned with in any model of simple RT.

Negative Findings

In assessing the value of any model or theory, it is incumbent upon the reviewer to take into account any negative findings as well as the positive findings. Thus far, we have considered in some detail the available evidence that appears to support the proposed model of simple RT and of the role played by the EEG. Having thus built up the case in favor of our model, it is time now to examine the available evidence that may serve to refute it. This latter evidence deals mainly with the general question of the relationship between the EEG and behavior, and with the specific question of the relation of the RT to frequency of the EEG. Let us begin by reporting these two lines of available evidence and, following this, attempt a balanced appraisal.

Clinical experience as well as a variety of laboratory investigations (see, e.g., Rossi and Zanchetti, 1957) have demonstrated that alterations in the state of consciousness are usually associated with changes in the EEG. The evidence most commonly cited is the finding that the dominant frequency of the EEG changes profoundly as a person passes through the various stages of the sleep-wakefulness cycle. While awake and alert, the EEG is normally dominated by 8-13 Hz activity — the alpha rhythm. Moving in the direction of high-level alertness, faster frequencies — beta activity — may be seen to replace the alpha activity. On the other hand, frequency of the EEG decreases as the state of consciousness moves in the opposite direction. Thus, as a person becomes drowsy, the background activity contains theta waves or frequencies less than 8 Hz. Finally, in deep sleep, the EEG is dominated by very slow activity — frequencies less than 4 Hz; this is referred to as delta activity.

The concept that there is a continuum of EEG frequencies associated with the sleep-wakefulness continuum is essentially in harmony with our hypothesis of the EEG as the physiological manifestation of a gating cycle. Thus, as frequency of the EEG slows down when a person becomes drowsy and goes to sleep, the inter-gate interval becomes longer so that responses will become increasingly slower and more sluggish until finally they cease to occur. Despite its generality, however, apparent exceptions to the principle that impaired consciousness is associated with slow activity in the EEG have been reported in the literature. For example, Wikler (1952) reported that although dogs administered the drug morphine (and in another experiment atrophine) showed evidences of sleep-like slow activity in their EEGs, they appeared to be behaviorally alert. Wikler called the phenomenon a "pharmacologic dissociation" of behavior and EEG activity, and suggested that the brain mechanisms which regulate the EEG may be distinct from those which regulate the state of consciousness.

Mirsky and Cardon (1962) addressed the question of the relationship between EEG frequency and impaired consciousness using human subjects. They compared performance on the Continuous Performance Test (1) under normal conditions, (2) after their subjects were sleep deprived, and (3) following the administration of Chlorpromazine. Sleep deprivation produced marked impairment in performance — prolonged and omitted responses — and this finding was accompanied by the presence of slow activity in the EEG. On the other hand, while Chlorpromazine produced similar impairment in performance, the EEG showed only little change. Mirsky and Cardon argued that these findings suggested the presence of a relative dissociation of the behavioral and physiological effects of the drug. They noted that the effects of Chlorpromazine were similar to the drug effects reported by Wikler (1952) in the experiment that was mentioned earlier. In discussing these two experiments, Lacey (1967) interpreted them to represent a "complete contradiction" between the electrocortical and behavioral signs of activation.

Of more direct relevance to the model with which this chapter is concerned are the experiments reported by Boddy (1971). Two experiments were carried out in which period of the EEG was studied in relation to performance on a simple RT test. Boddy argued that measurements of EEG period based upon the tracings observed in the interval between stimulus and response presented problems as they might be contaminated by the sensory evoked potential that can sometimes be recorded in the raw EEG tracing. To avoid this problem, he analyzed samples of the EEG that were obtained at other times. Thus, in his first experiment, the measurements of EEG period were based upon a one-minute sample of the subjects' resting EEGs. The correlation between auditory RT and EEG period in twelve subjects was 0.37; this coefficient was not statistically significant. A replication using seventeen subjects yielded a correlation coefficient of only 0.05. In his second experiment, EEG period measurements were made from the tracings recorded in the one-second intervals immediately prior to the occurrence of the stimuli. The correlation between auditory RT and EEG period in twenty subjects was 0.21, while the correlation between visual RT and EEG period in the same sample was 0.26. Neither of these correlation coefficients was statistically significant. Intra-individual correlation coefficients were also computed and their mean values estimated. Like the other coefficients reported by Boddy, these were in the predicted direction; but again, they were not statistically significant.

Shagass, Straumanis, and Overton (1972) have also reported a study in which performance on a simple RT task was investigated in relation to a period of the EEG as measured in a one-second sample preceeding the occurrence of the stimulus. This experiment, which measured RT to a light flash, employed a tone as a warning signal and was performed on thirty-five normal young adults as well as on a heterogeneous group of thirty-eight hospitalized young psychiatric patients. These investigators converted their EEG period measurements to frequency, and reported correlations between RT and EEG frequency of –0.16 and –0.12, respectively, in the normal subjects and the hospitalized patients. As in the earlier-mentioned study, by Boddy, the correlations were in the direction predicted by our model. But again, they were not statistically significant.

Appraisal

It is clear that the usefulness of the proposed model of simple reaction time stands or falls on the reliability of the evidence concerning the relationship between EEG frequency and the sleep-wakefulness continuum in general, and between EEG period and RT in particular. In this writer's opinion, the evidence concerning the dissociation of the behavioral from the EEG effects of certain drugs is far from being convincing. There are two reasons. In the first place, the evidence from the animal studies is mainly anecdotal. For example, Wikler (1952) had no quantitative measure of the animal's behavior recorded contiguously with the EEG data. The need for working quantitatively is obvious; side-by-side recording of the EEG and behavior is important as it is well-known to clinical electroencephalographers that transient shifts from wakefulness to drowsiness and sleep can be very rapid indeed. Some EEGs may even show features of wakefulness and Stage II sleep within a few seconds of each other. In studies where behavior was quantified and EEG recordings were made contiguously with recordings of behavior—as in Volavka, Levine, Feldstein, and Fink's (1974) study of the effects of heroin in man—the results showed an association of EEG frequency with behavior, not a dissociation.

Secondly, adherents to the concept of dissociation between EEG and behavior seem at times, to assume that behavior must be completely determined by the EEG if the EEG is to play any role in its production. In other words, the idea that multiple factors might be involved seems sometimes to be ignored. To cite a specific example, suppose administration of a particular drug results in impaired performance on a task that is similar to the impairment produced by, say, sleep deprivation. But we find that, while the EEG undergoes profound changes with sleep deprivation, the drug in question has little or no effect on the EEG. Does this mean that there is a dissociation between EEG and behavior? Hardly, for we surely cannot admit this to be the only possibility. The behavior under investigation may be determined by a number of factors with the EEG being only one of those involved. In the case of our model of RT, the drug in question may have no effect whatever on frequency of the gating signal. But it may markedly reduce transmission system excitability instead; and, in so doing, it could prolong the RT by an amount comparable to that observed during sleep deprivation. Clearly, the results of the present inquiry argue against the idea that a single factor can account for all the variance in even the simplest behavior.

Turning now to the RT studies themselves, it is interesting to note that all the correlation coefficients between EEG and simple RT that have been reported in the literature from group data are in the direction predicted by our model. Thus, although the coefficients differ greatly in magnitude and some are not even statistically significant, all correlations reported between EEG period and RT have been positive while those between EEG frequency and RT are negative. But why should there be such a large difference in magnitude? If the proposed model has merit, why should some of the correlation coefficients reported be so small?

To begin with, it is well-known that restricting the range of either of the correlated variables will reduce the size of the correlation coefficient. The two studies cited earlier by Surwillo employed adults aged 28-99 years (Surwillo, 1963a, b) and children aged 4-17 years (Surwillo, 1971). EEG period is known to change profoundly during the course of growth and development and also in old age. Note in Table I of the present chapter that the range was 84-144 msec in the adult subjects and 88-138 msec in children. So in these experiments, period of the EEG varied over a relatively wide range. On the other hand, Boddy's (1971) second experiment used young adults aged 18-38 years as subjects; EEG period in this group had a range of only 91-117 msec. The range in the first experiment was not reported. Shagass, Straumanis, and Overton (1972) used young adults as well; EEG periods for their subjects were not reported.

Another factor that needs to be considered is the methodology employed in the different studies. In the experiments reported by Surwillo, estimates of EEG period always were made from EEG tracings recorded in the interval between stimulus and response. There was good reason for doing this. We have hypothesized that the EEG is the physiological manifestation of a central gating mechanism, with each wave in the tracing representing a gating cycle. Because EEG period is not a constant but shows considerable wave-to-wave variation within an individual, simple logic would demand that—in testing this theory—our estimates of EEG period be made from tracings that are temporally contiguous with the behavior under investigation. The gating signals present while the subject is merely resting can hardly be expected to play an essential or even important role in the subject's performance taking place at an entirely different time. Despite this, however, in his first experiment Boddy (1971) correlated measures of RT with estimates of EEG period that were obtained from tracings taken at another time while the subjects were resting.

In Boddy's second experiment, the EEG data at least were obtained during performance of the RT task. But the RT and EEG data still were not temporally contiguous. In that experiment, EEG periods were estimated from one second samples preceding the initiation of the stimuli. Shagass, Straumanis, and Overton (1972) used the same design. Because the measurements of RT and EEG period in these experiments were not contiguous in time, it would appear that these studies are not valid tests of the proposed model.

It is true, of course, that the possibility exists for the sensory evoked potential to contaminate the spontaneous electrical activity recorded in the interval between stimulus and response. This apparently was Boddy's rationale for taking the EEG measurements prior to the initiation of the stimulus. But the evoked potential is rarely visible in the raw EEG record; moreover, if present it usually is of very low amplitude in the recordings from electrodes located at a distance from the midline. Nevertheless, the occasional presence of a sensory evoked potential in the raw EEG would add error to the estimate of EEG period, thereby reducing the magnitude of the correlation between RT and EEG period. The effect on the correlations based on the group data would be minimal as the values correlated are averages. But in the case of the correlations within individuals, a few aberrant values in the distribution of EEG period measurements could significantly alter the size of the correlation coefficient or even its sign.

An important factor affecting the correlations between RT and EEG period within individual subjects is the presence of variations in the subjects' attention level during performance of the test. It is well-known that a drop in a person's level of attention can significantly lengthen the RT— sometimes more than double its value. In Chapter 4, we discussed the topic of attention and formulated a hypothesis concerning the brain mechanisms involved. Attention, we said, was equivalent in physiological terms to bringing the gating signal—the central timing mechanism—to bear on some specific neural circuit or group of circuits. In the case at hand, this involves connecting up the *b* neurons in our model of simple RT to the source of the gating signal. With this done, the circuits become functional and a response to the stimulus will occur in the shortest possible time commensurate with the frequency of the gating signals and the excitability level of the transmission system. On the other hand, if the attention is not focused on the task, or has wandered away from it momentarily, one or more gating signals may go by unused by the circuit until the attention is again redirected to the task. The result, of course, is a prolonged RT.

Consider a simple example: Let us assume, as we did earlier in the case of the example in Figure 30, that the afferent and efferent delays for our model amount to a total of 80 msec. Suppose, also, that the attention is directed upon the task and that the EEG at the time has a frequency of 8 Hz which is equivalent to a period of 120 msec. Under these conditions, RT could be equal to $80 + 120 = 200$ msec. But, now, suppose that the frequency of the EEG increases to 12 Hz so that the period becomes equal to 83 msec. If the attention continued to be focused on the task, we should predict that a shorter RT would result, namely, $80 + 83 = 163$ msec. This is as would be predicted by our model. However, suppose instead that the attention wandered away from the task so that the upcoming gating signal went by unused and the circuit had to wait until the next gating signal came along. In such a case, RT would be equal to $80 + 2 \times 83 = 246$ msec, or 46 msec longer than it was when EEG frequency was 8 Hz, or 4 Hz slower. It is easy to see from this simple example how an individual's correlation between EEG period and RT could become zero or even negative if his/her attention was allowed to wander during performance of the task.

When considered in its entirety, therefore, the bulk of the available evidence seems to be in favor of there being a relationship between simple RT and EEG frequency, with faster frequencies going along with shorter RTs and vice versa. Variations in the strength of this relationship appear to be attributable to a variety of factors that prolong RT and contribute to its variability, as well as to conditions that restrict the range of the EEG frequency. As we have seen, this relationship and the model in the context of which it has been discussed are capable of accounting for many of the findings that have been reported in the RT literature. In the next chapter, we turn to the question of what happens when the excitability of the component elements that make up the model is taken into account. An important aspect of this question concerns the effects of stimuli that are closely spaced in time.

CHAPTER 7

SIMPLE REACTION TIME AND THE ROLE OF TRANSMISSION SYSTEM EXCITABILITY

I N THE LAST chapter, we noted that one source of variability in the RT is the excitability of the neurons that make up the models we have been discussing. For the sake of simplicity, however, we disregarded this factor and assumed that the neurons involved were always maximally excitable whenever an adequate stimulus was present. This assumption, of course, is far from the truth. As mentioned in Chapter 3, neurons are refractory for an interval following stimulation at which time their excitability may be profoundly affected. In this chapter, therefore, we consider the role played by excitability differences in the functioning of our models of simple RT.

Excitability and Recovery Period

Immediately following a response to stimulation, a neuron typically is incapable of responding a second time. This is the so-called absolute refractory period; if a stimulus occurs during this period of time it will not elicit a response. Unless some device is employed to prolong the stimulus until the neuron has recovered, the stimulus is lost for all practical purposes. The process of recovery, therefore, is not instantaneous but takes time. Excitability is only gradually restored, and the interval during which this takes place is referred to as the relative refractory period. The duration of these events, that is, the time that elapses between a response and total recovery from the response, is referred to as the *recovery* or *refractory period*. From this it is obvious that excitability varies according to how far along the way recovery has progressed.

107

Recovery Period and the Cortical Gating Cycle

As we have seen in earlier chapters, the gating signal is a critical factor in the design of our models of simple RT. Indeed, information cannot move from one processing stage to another nor can a response be initiated in the absence of a gating signal. But now, suppose that one of the elements in our model is refractory when the effects of a stimulus arrive there along with a gating signal. By way of example, suppose that neuron a in the model of simple RT seen in Figure 23 happens to be in a refractory state when the gating signal comes along in neuron b_2. What will take place? It is obvious that the gating signal will go by unused if neuron a has not recovered sufficiently for the combined effect at the synapse of activity in neuron b_2 and in the output of the integrator circuit to fire it. In other words, the gating signal will be impotent if the recovery period happens to be longer than the time since the previous gating signal. Whenever this occurs, the response will be delayed until neuron a has recovered sufficiently and another gating signal comes along later.

It will be seen, therefore, that duration of the recovery period itself is not the important variable in the functioning of our models but rather duration of the recovery period *in relation to the time between consecutive gating signals*. This is shown graphically in Figure 41 where the number of units of information processed by a circuit like our simple RT model is shown in relation to the recovery period and the inter-gate interval. In the two examples on the left side of Figure 41, the duration of the recovery or refractory period is less than the time between consecutive gating signals. The excitability recovery cycle or the rate of recovery from previous stimulation is the same in both cases. Note, however, that the cortical gating cycle—that is to say, the time between consecutive gating signals or the inter-gate interval—is different. Cortical gating cycle is longer in the example shown in the lower half of the figure than in the example shown in the upper half. These are the same as the conditions stipulated for our model in Figure 26 (Chapter 6).

Under the stated conditions, processing time in both these examples will be determined solely by the duration of the inter-gate intervals. In Chapter 3 we suggested that the inter-gate interval is the *time quantum* in our models, that is, the minimum time necessary for a circuit to process a single unit of information. If this is so, then three units of information will be processed in both of the cases seen at the left in Figure 41; but

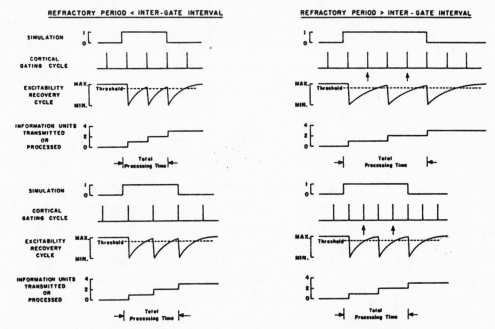

Figure 41: Effect of transmission system excitability on information processing in relation to the cortical gating cycle. Reprint of Figure 1 from Surwillo, W.W.: *Biological Psychology*, 1975, *3*, 247-261, by courtesy of the North-Holland Publishing Company.

because the cortical gating cycle is longer in the example shown below, the total processing time is correspondingly longer.

Turning now to the two examples on the right side of Figure 41, we see what happens when the refractory period is longer than the inter-gate interval. The example in the upper half shows a cortical gating cycle of the same duration as in the example on the left side of the figure. But recovery from stimulation takes approximately twice as long. Under these conditions, two of the gating signals (marked by the vertical arrows) are unused so that processing of the three units of information is delayed by the equivalent of two gating cycles. The example in the lower half on the right side of Figure 41 also shows two gating signals going by unused, but not because recovery from stimulation takes longer. In this case, recovery from stimulation occurs at the same rate as in the corresponding example at the left. However, these gating signals are impotent because the inter-gate interval is so short that excitability has not sufficiently recovered in time for the next gating signal that comes along.

Thus, when duration of the recovery period is longer than the inter-gate interval — or, to put it another way, when the ratio of recovery period to inter-gate interval is greater than one — some gating signals will be impotent and will go by unused during processing. This ratio can become greater than one either by making the recovery period longer or, alternatively, by making the inter-gate interval shorter. Whichever the case, the net result is to prolong processing time and in the instance of our models of simple RT, increase the RT.

Excitability or Attention?

The reader will recognize that the results of prolonging the recovery period are similar to the effects produced by a reduction in attention during performance of the reaction task. The effects of fluctuations in attention were discussed in the last chapter. Note, however, that there is a major difference between the two phenomena. For the case in which excitability is the significant factor, gating signals are actually present in the b neurons but some of them go by without being used in processing. On the other hand, gating signals are not even present in the b neurons when the attention is directed away from the task. But in testing out our model, how do we decide which phenomenon is operating? In a particular case at hand, are the responses prolonged because the attention is wandering or are they prolonged because of a lengthening of the recovery period?

Some data already mentioned in Chapter 6 (see Table I) reported that simple RT in a group of 110 normal children 4-17 years old varied markedly with age. While RT was hardly more than 200 msec in the 16 and 17 year olds, it was 500 msec and longer in the 5 and 6 year olds. The finding of a significant correlation between RT and EEG period was, as we noted earlier, evidence in support of our proposed models of simple RT. But a partial regression analysis revealed that the difference in EEG period associated with age during growth and development was capable of accounting for barely 9 percent of the total variance in the RT associated with age (Surwillo, 1971). Clearly, some other factor or factors were responsible for the markedly longer RTs of the young children. As this study had been carefully designed to assure that all the subjects were alert and attending to the task during performance, it hardly seemed possible that the prolonged RTs of the younger subjects could be attributable to a lack of attention. From the standpoint of our model, this suggested that a prolonged recovery period might be the primary factor involved.

The Time Quantum

Earlier, we hypothesized that the posterior dominant rhythm of the EEG is the physiological manifestation of the gating signal. If this is so, then each full wave or some fraction thereof (half wave or quarter wave) corresponds to a cortical gating cycle which, in turn, represents a time quantum according to which the events taking place in our model are clocked. In the light of the discussion of the previous section, we should expect to see a stepwise increase in the number of quanta that enter into a response as the recovery period becomes longer.

Similar speculations about a time quantum in the central nervous system have been offered by Stroud (1949) and White (1963) in reviewing the concept of psychological duration. Michon (1965) has assembled evidence for the quantum-like character of the perception of duration, with the quanta reportedly varying between 50 and 100 msec. In harmony with this finding, Kristofferson (1967) presented evidence from which he concluded that duration of the time quantum is equal to the duration of a half-wave of the alpha rhythm of the EEG.

Assuming that Kristofferson's (1967) conclusion is correct, we counted the number of half waves recorded in the interval between stimulus and response during performance of the simple RT experiment; we then plotted the average number of half waves against age. Data for the children came from the study mentioned in the last section (Surwillo, 1971), while the data for adults were obtained from an earlier investigation (Surwillo, 1964b). For the adults, only an overall group mean is shown because there was no relationship between the number of half waves and age of these subjects. The outcome is shown as the solid circles in Figure 42. The open circles are similar data for a disjunctive RT task or reaction task in which the subject has to make a decision before responding; in this case, high and low tones presented at random were the stimuli and the subjects were instructed to respond only to the high tones. These latter data will be taken up in a later chapter.

The solid circles in Figure 42 show that, as age of the children increases, there is a rapid decrease in the number of half waves that enter into the response until about age 140 months. Thereafter, the number of half waves is substantially unchanged with increasing age, remaining at about 5 half waves throughout adulthood and old age. Visual inspection suggests that the data may follow a decaying exponential function; but a statistical test revealed that they·did not fit an exponential equation. However, when log log values of average number of half waves were plotted against age, the resulting curve was linear for ages less than 140 months. This finding is interesting not only because it suggests a possible relation of these data to the Gompertz function of biological growth but also because 140 months, or approximately 11.5 years, represents a

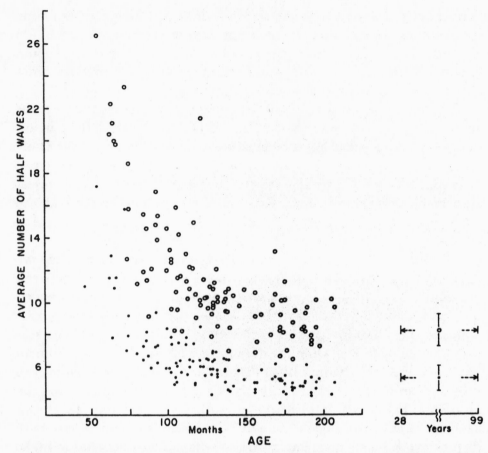

Figure 42: Average number of EEG half waves recorded in the interval between stimulus and response in a simple RT (solid circles) and a disjunctive RT (open circles) task across the age span from 3.5-99 years. Limits shown are ±σ values. Copyright© 1971, The Society for Psychophysiological Research. Reprinted with permission of the publisher from Surwillo, W.W.: Human reaction time and period of the EEG in relation to development. *Psychophysiology*, 1971, *8*, 468-482, Figure 6.

critical stage in Piaget's scheme of human intellectual development. Thus, according to Piaget's scheme, the transition to "formally operational intelligence," which is the last of his four chronological stages in the development of intelligence, occurs at or beyond the eleventh year (Flavell, 1963).

But let us return to the original question that concerned us. Figure 42 suggests that the number of time quanta needed to process the same amount of information decreases with age during growth and development; the number is markedly larger in young children. Considering the systematic nature of this change, it would be surprising indeed if a factor like attention were responsible. For this reason, we focussed instead on the possibility of transmission system excitability being the major responsible factor. We hypothesized, therefore, that the rate of recovery of excitability following stimulation is slower in young than in older children and increases during growth and development so that fewer time quanta go unused during information processing as a child grows into adolescence and adulthood. But in order to test this hypothesis, some way had to be found of measuring excitability or, alternatively, of estimating the time it takes for the information processing system to recover from previous stimulation.

Measuring Excitability — The Method of Closely-Spaced Stimuli

Measurement of physiological excitability appears to date back to the late 19th century when a refractory phase was discovered in cardiac tissue. By the end of the 19th century, Broca and Richet (1897) found that nervous tissue also displayed a refractory period, with the motor centers of the cerebral cortex of the dog showing a refractory period of about 0.1 sec to electrical stimulation. In the first of a long series of studies, Lucas (1909) and Lucas and Adrian (1917) investigated the refractory phase in nerve and skeletal muscle. Pairs of closely-spaced stimuli were employed, and the consistent finding was an increased latency of response to the stimulus that was applied during the time interval closely following the previous stimulation. Lucas (1911) suggested that the amount by which the response to the second stimulus of a pair was prolonged could be used to estimate the excitability which is left in the wake of the previous stimulation.

The Psychological Refractory Period — Historical Background

Telford (1931) was the first to attempt measurement of the recovery period of the more complex processes that are encountered in voluntary behavior. In a landmark study, Telford used Lucas' method of closely-spaced stimuli in a simple RT experiment. Pairs of stimuli having inter-stimulus intervals of different duration were presented to alert subjects with the instruction to respond to both stimuli of the pairs as quickly as possible. The inter-stimulus intervals used were 0.5, 1, 2, and 4 sec; they occurred in equal numbers and were presented in random order. For inter-stimulus intervals equal to 1, 2, and 4 sec, the mean RTs to the second stimulus of the pairs ranged between 241 and 276 msec. On the other hand, when the inter-stimulus interval was only 0.5 sec, the RT was significantly prolonged, with the mean value being equal to 335 msec. Telford attributed the prolonged RT to the effects of a "psychological refractory period."

In the ensuing years, Telford's finding was amply confirmed. By the early 50s, Welford (1952) concluded that in experiments using closely-spaced stimuli, RT and duration of the inter-stimulus interval usually showed an inverse relationship, with RT to the second stimulus becoming longer as the inter-stimulus interval takes on values that are successively shorter than 500 msec. Some later investigations of the psychological refractory period showed that the inverse relationship held even if no response was required to the first stimulus of the pair (Bertelson, 1967; Bertelson and Tisseyre, 1968, 1969; Davis, 1962; Fraisse, 1957; Kay and Weiss, 1961; Nickerson, 1965). Under these conditions, the delays in RT were considerably shorter and the effect did not show itself until the inter-stimulus interval was 100 msec or less. This finding was important as it suggested that the prolonged RT observed to accompany the short-duration, inter-stimulus intervals could not be attributable purely to the motor component of the response. The relationship, moreover, has proven to be very robust, having survived a determined effort on the part of Gottsdanker and Stelmach (1971) to eliminate it through training and practice at the task.

The Single-Channel Concept

It was suggested earlier that the markedly longer RTs observed in children 10 years and younger may be due, in major part, to a reduced excitability level associated with a lengthened recovery period following stimulation. In proposing this explanation, we are assuming as a general principle that the waking brain is continually, ceaselessly processing information. With specific regard to our model of simple RT, we also assume that the circuitry involved has a limited capacity for processing that information. Thus, any signals that may be present get fed into the input and are processed by the comparator whether or not they have any significance as stimuli, as long as the channel is not being used by another signal at the same time. If more than one signal occurs during the same cortical gating cycle, the signal occurring later would have to be put into storage and then fed in for processing on the next cycle that the channel was free.

These ideas are incorporated into what has come to be known as the single-channel hypothesis of information processing. While it is thought that a number of operations concerned in information processing can work in parallel, the concept of serial processing and the single-channel hypothesis has considerable currency. Its basic tenet is that the capacity to process information is limited ultimately to a single channel; that somewhere along the line of central mechanisms from sensory input to effector output there is at least one mechanism that can deal with only one signal at a time (Welford, 1980). Figure 43 is a model showing our version of this hypothesis.

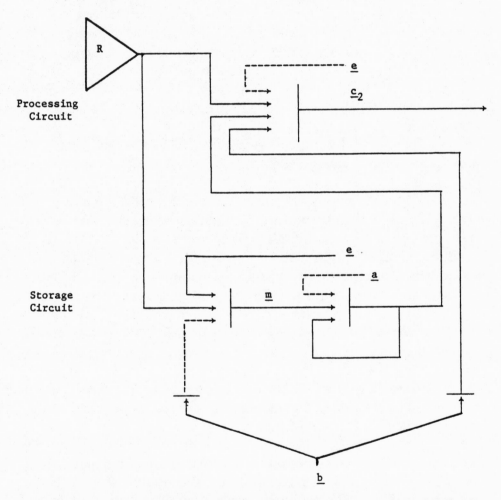

Figure 43: A simple storage and switching system for processing closely-spaced stimuli or stimuli falling within a single cortical gating cycle. Neuron c_2 corresponds to the input neuron and a the output neuron (inhibitory component) of the model in Figure 23 of Chapter 5, while neuron e is the output neuron of an integrator circuit like that shown in Figure 21, also of Chapter 5. Dashed lines are inhibitory, solid lines excitatory neurons.

A Practical Model

Figure 43 illustrates one way in which the model of simple RT that was described in Figure 23 of Chapter 5 could be modified to handle the processing of closely-spaced stimuli. The circuit in Figure 43 should be perused in conjunction with that shown in Figure 23 in order to understand how it functions. Note that the circuit is divided into two separate segments, one devoted to processing and the other to storage. The receptor is connected to both: to the processing segment via the synapse of neuron c_2 and to the storage segment via the synapse of neuron m. Neuron c_2 is biased to fire when two elements at the synapse are simultaneously active, while neuron m fires when one element is active. The presence of gating signals (activity in b) has an excitatory effect on c_2 but an inhibitory effect on m. On the other hand, activity in e, the output neuron from the integrator circuit of the model, has an inhibitory effect on c_2 but an excitatory effect on m. Finally, neuron a is an inhibitory neuron fired by activity in the output neuron (excitatory neuron a) in the Figure 23 model.

Given these conditions, let us assume that R, the receptor, has been stimulated and that a gating signal appears in neuron b. With the neurons from R and b simultaneously active, c_2 will fire and the algorithm described in Chapter 5 for identifying a signal as the stimulus will be implemented. As the b neuron impinging on neuron m is inhibitory, it will cancel the excitatory effect of the R neuron at this synapse so that neuron m will be silent. The decision that the signal processed by comparator and integrator really is a stimulus is distinguished by the firing of neuron e, the output neuron of the integrator circuit. Since its effect on the synapse of c_2 is inhibitory, neuron e cancels any remaining excitatory effect of the R neuron so that c_2 stops firing. At the same time, the excitatory branch of neuron e cancels the residual effects of the inhibitory neuron at the synapse of neuron m so that a signal closely following the first and impinging on R fires m. This second signal thereupon is held in store by the reverberating, short-term memory circuit until the next (the second) gating signal comes along and the information is sent on to neuron c_2 for processing.

Some interesting predictions may be made from this model. In the first place, it will be apparent that the RT to the second signal, if it is indeed identified as a stimulus, will be longer than the RT to a signal that occurs by itself. By how much time the response is delayed will depend upon the amount of time that the signal is held in store. This time, of course, will vary depending upon the temporal location of the signal with reference to the phase of the gating cycle. If the signals in the reaction task are presented at random so they show no preference with respect to any phase of the gating cycle, we should expect on the average, that the RT would be prolonged by a time approximately equal to one-half the duration of a gating cycle.

A second prediction from the model is concerned with what takes place if neuron c_2 should happen to be refractory following stimulation by the first signal so it cannot be fired when the second gating signal comes along. Under such conditions, information processing will be interrupted and will have to wait until neuron c_2 has recovered and the next or third gating signal comes along. When, finally, the comparison with the standard is carried out and a response is signalled, the activity in the inhibitory neuron fired by output neuron *a* cancels the excitatory effect of the feedback neuron in the storage circuit. This operation clears the storage circuit thereby making it available for future use. The final result of the storage operation and the lengthened recovery period is an RT that, on the average, will be prolonged by about one and one-half cortical gating cycles.

Closely-Spaced Signals and RT in Children and Adults

In order to test the model just described, a reaction task employing closely-spaced signals was used with two different groups of subjects; one group consisted of 13 adults aged 19-29 years (mean = 23.1 years) while the other consisted of 13 children aged 8-11 years (mean = 9.4 years). Children 11 years and younger were chosen for this study because the data in Figure 42 suggested that recovery of excitability following stimulation would be slower in these persons than in older children and adults. The subjects performed a reaction task in which the signals were clicks; the experiment involved presenting a total of 96 sequences of 3 clicks each, in each of 4 separate sessions. Each sequence consisted of a soft click that served as a warning signal followed, after an interval, by a pair of loud clicks. The foreperiod, or time between warning signal and first loud click, varied at random between 3 and 4.6 sec in increments of 0.2 sec; the loud clicks were separated by inter-stimulus intervals of 50, 100, 250, 500, 750, and 1,000 msec, in equal numbers, presented at random.[1] Subjects were instructed to listen for the soft click

---

[1] The purpose of including inter-stimulus intervals that were longer than one-half second, was methodological. By doing so, we hoped to increase the temporal uncertainty of the second loud click of the pairs. For this reason, the data obtained for the inter-stimulus intervals of 750 and 1,000 msec were not analyzed.

which warned them that a pair of loud clicks was coming up, and then to respond to the second loud click, as quickly as possible, by pushing a button.

We expected the inter-stimulus interval of 50 msec in this experiment
to be a critical value. Given that the time quantum or cortical gating cycle is equal to the duration of a half wave of the posterior-dominant
rhythm of the EEG, an inter-stimulus interval of 50 msec would, at
times, be less than the cortical gating cycle. This means that the second
click would need to be stored until the first click had cleared the processing circuit. The anticipated result is a prolonged RT, longer on the
average by about 25 msec than the RT to clicks following the longer
inter-stimulus intervals. Figure 44 reveals that this was indeed the case.

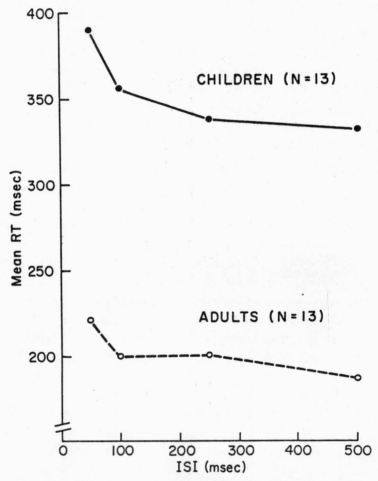

Figure 44: RT to the second of two closely-spaced clicks in relation to the inter-stimulus interval (ISI) in children and adults. Copyright© 1976, John Wiley & Sons, Inc. Reprinted by permission of John Wiley & Sons, Inc. from Surwillo, W.W. and Titus, T.G.: Reaction time and
the psychological refractory period in children and adults. *Developmental Psychobiology*, 1976, *9*,
517-527, Figure 1.

For the adult subjects, mean RT to the clicks following the 50 msec inter-stimulus interval was about 25 msec longer than the average of the RTs to the clicks following the longer inter-stimulus intervals of 100, 250, and 500 msec.

The curve shown in Figure 44 for the children's data is also in agreement with our hypothesis and is likewise in accord with our model. An analysis of variance revealed not only that children had longer RTs than adults and that their RTs increased as duration of inter-stimulus interval decreased, but also that children showed larger increases in RT with decreasing inter-stimulus interval than adults. This latter finding, of course, is compatible with the view that recovery of excitability following stimulation takes longer in children than in adults. Compared with the RTs to the clicks following inter-stimulus intervals of 250 and 500 msec, the RT to the clicks following the 50 msec interval were somewhat longer than the duration of a cortical gating cycle. In the context of our model and the hypothesis under investigation, this finding is compatible with the idea that one time quantum went by unused by the children during the processing operation.

Although the results of this experiment are clearly in support of our model, it is important to recognize that the overall difference accounted for by one unused quantum is only about one-third of the actual difference observed between the RTs of children and adults. Note, however, that if the recovery periods of other elements or stages in the information-processing chain were also sufficiently longer in children so that additional gating signals were unused, the overall processing-time difference between children and adults would be even greater. For example, two additional gating signals going unused in an additional processing stage would result in the children's RTs being longer than those of adults by the duration of an additional two cortical gating cycles. However, while clearly plausible, this view goes far beyond presently-available data and is, therefore, purely speculative. Hopefully, other experiments yet to be done will be able to provide more evidence and further insight into this question.

Recapitulation

Our model of simple RT, therefore emerges as a three-factor model. RT is determined by three parameters, namely, (1) the duration of the cortical gating cycle, (2) the phase of the cortical gating cycle in which a stimulus happens to fall, and (3) the rate of recovery of excitability following stimulation of the transmission elements. In Chapter 6 and also in the present chapter, evidence has been marshalled in support of the model. As we have seen, the cortical gating cycle possesses a degree of physiological reality insofar as it may be defined by the frequency of the posterior-dominant rhythm of the EEG. Recovery period, on the other hand, has merely been inferred from behavioral data, being estimated from the changes in RT associated with inter-stimulus intervals of different duration in an experiment using closely-spaced stimuli.

Obviously, we cannot have a truly psychophysiological model of simple RT unless physiological methods of measuring the recovery of cortical functioning from stimulation are available. For this reason, some preliminary experiments that address this important topic have been carried out. The findings of this research are taken up in the next two sections.

Physiological Measures of Cortical Excitability — Cortical Evoked Response Recovery Functions

Gastaut, Gastaut, Roger, Corriol, and Naquet (1951) were among the first to make use of physiological methods to obtain an estimate of cortical excitability. In their classic experiment, the electrical response of the cerebral cortex evoked by peripheral stimulation was recorded using scalp electrodes. As a stimulus, the experiment used two closely-spaced, bright flashes of light in which the interval between flashes was varied from trial to trial. The investigators reported that the cortical response to the second, or test flash varied in amplitude as a function of the time between the two flashes. The relative size of the response to the second flash, compared to the size of the response evoked by the first or conditioning flash, was taken as an index of cortical excitability.

Later, Cigánek (1964) and Schwartz and Shagass (1964) used the technique of coherent signal averaging[2] in conjunction with the method of closely-spaced stimuli to plot the time course of the cortical recovery cycle to peripheral stimulation. To do this, the evoked electrical response of the cortex was obtained to a single stimulus (S_1) and then to a pair of stimuli $(S_2 + S_3)$, each element of which was identical to the single stimulus. S_2 was well separated from S_1 so that any recovery period attributable to S_1 was over before S_2 came along. For each trial, an estimate of

---

[2]Coherent signal averaging is a computer technique that adds together the electrical responses to many identical stimuli for the purpose of enhancing the response to the stimulus and reducing or "averaging out" any unwanted background signals or noise.

the cortical response to S_3 was obtained by automatic subtraction, a computer technique in which R_1, the response to the single stimulus, was subtracted from $(R_2 + R_3)$, the response to the pair of closely-spaced stimuli. The individual trials thereupon were averaged to yield the average cortical evoked response to S_3. This procedure could be repeated for pairs of stimuli having different inter-stimulus intervals, and the resulting data were used to generate cortical evoked response recovery functions.

Cortical evoked responses, of course, are involuntary phenomena. They display a complex waveform consisting of a number of different components that are thought to represent the arrival of information at different areas of the brain and to reflect the serial transfer of information between successive brain regions (John and Schwartz, 1978). A wide variety of investigations have suggested that some components in the cortical evoked response may be associated with information processing per se (e.g., Bergamini and Bergamasco, 1967; Donchin and Lindsley, 1969; Regan, 1972; Shagass, 1972). For this reason, an experiment was performed (Surwillo, 1977a) in which cortical evoked response recovery functions and the RT were obtained in the same subjects. The purpose of this study was to find out if the cortical evoked response to the second of two closely-spaced stimuli varies with the inter-stimulus interval in the same way that the RT varies with the inter-stimulus interval in the case of voluntary responses.

The stimuli used in this investigation were clicks similar to those employed in the experiment that was discussed in the last section. The clicks occurred in sequences, with a sequence consisting of three clicks of equal loudness. First came a single click (S_1) followed after a variable interval of several seconds by a pair of closely-spaced clicks ($S_2 + S_3$). The two clicks of the pairs were separated by intervals of 50, 100, 250, 500, 750, and 1,000 msec in equal numbers, varying at random. Cortical evoked responses were obtained to S_1 and to ($S_2 + S_3$), and automatic subtraction and coherent signal averaging by computer were used to yield the average evoked response to S_3.

Some of the coherently-averaged cortical electrical responses evoked by the single clicks (S_1), as recorded from scalp electrodes, are shown in Figure 45. These cortical evoked responses were obtained, in each case, by averaging the responses to a total of 50 clicks. They are typical of the tracings recorded in response to auditory stimulation. The waveforms nicely show the three most prominent intermediate-latency components designated P_1, N_1, and P_2, where P defines the most prominent positive deflections and N the most prominent negative deflection.

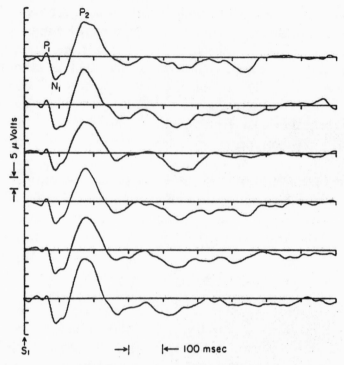

Figure 45: Average cortical evoked responses to single clicks (71 dB peak level) recorded from the vertex (Cz in the "10-20" International System) using linked-ears reference. Each tracing is based upon an average of 50 responses. Positive is up. Copyright© 1977, The Society for Psychophysiological Research. Reprinted with permission of the publisher from Surwillo, W.W.: Cortical evoked response recovery functions: Physiological manifestations of the psychological refractory period? *Psychophysiology,* 1977, *14,* 32-39, Figure 1.

In Figure 46 we have the average cortical evoked responses to S_3, the second of the closely-spaced clicks, in relation to the duration of the inter-stimulus interval. These data come from one of the subjects tested. Note that the latencies of the three most prominent components of the evoked responses appear to be prolonged as the two clicks in the pairs move closer together. The finding is clearly suggestive of a refractory period being involved in the phenomenon. This impression was corroborated by the group data.

Figure 47 shows the latencies of the three most prominent components of the average cortical evoked responses plotted as a function of the inter-stimulus interval. These curves are averages of data taken from 12 normal young adults who served as the subjects in the study. It is apparent that the latencies of the various components of the responses to the single clicks are very nearly identical for all the different sequences, whereas the latencies to the second click of the pairs increase as the

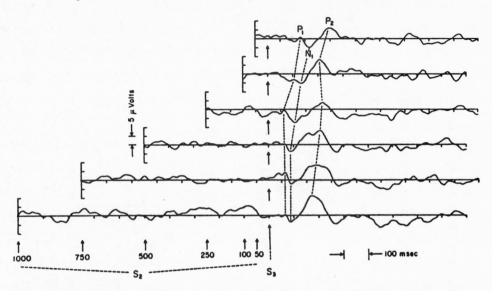

Figure 46: Average cortical evoked responses to the second click (S$_3$) of a pair of closely-spaced clicks (S$_2$+S$_3$), recorded from the vertex using linked-ears reference. Clicks are all 71 dB peak level. The six tracings, which correspond to click pairs having inter-stimulus intervals of 50, 100, 250, 500, 750, and 1,000 msec, respectively from top to bottom, have been shifted along the horizontal axis so that all S$_3$s coincide. Positive is up, and each tracing is based upon an average of 50 responses. Copyright© 1977, The Society for Psychophysiological Research. Reprinted with permission of the publisher from Surwillo, W.W.: Cortical evoked response recovery functions: Physiological manifestations of the psychological refractory period? *Psychophysiology*, 1977, *14*, 32-39, Figure 3.

inter-stimulus interval decreases. This finding was statistically significant by analysis of variance at the .01 level of confidence for the P$_1$ and P$_2$ components but not in the case of the N$_1$ component. Figure 47 also shows how RT varies in relation to inter-stimulus interval in the same 12 subjects. These data were collected in a separate experiment.[3] The curve for RT shows that the subject's voluntary responses were prolonged as the duration of the inter-stimulus interval increased. This finding, which was statistically significant at the .01 level of confidence, is in agreement with data already reported in Figure 44 and discussed earlier in the present chapter.

The foregoing evidence suggests that the physiological and behavioral phenomena covary; that the cortical evoked response recovery function may be a physiological manifestation of the psychological

---

[3]Problems with artifacts due primarily to blinking and involuntary eye movements during performance of the reaction task made it impossible to collect the physiological and behavioral data in the same experiment.

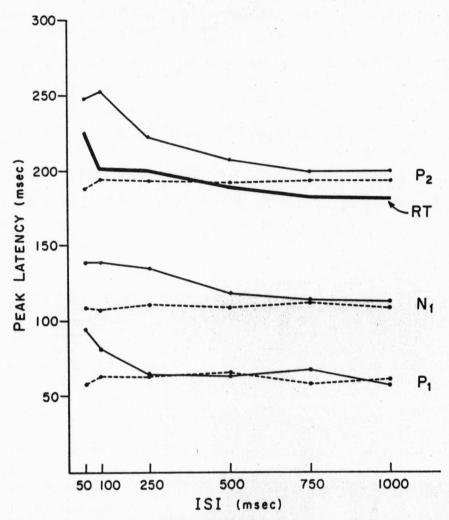

Figure 47: Latency of the P_1, N_1, and P_2 components of the average cortical evoked responses and reaction time (RT), all plotted as a function of the duration of the inter-stimulus interval (ISI). Dashed lines are data from evoked responses to single clicks; solid lines, data from evoked responses to the second click of the pairs of clicks; heavy solid line, RTs to the second click of the pairs. RTs were obtained in a separate experiment. All data are means from 12 young adults. Copyright© 1977, The Society for Psychophysiological Research. Reprinted with permission of the publisher from Surwillo, W.W.: Cortical evoked response recovery functions: Physiological manifestations of the psychological refractory period? *Psychophysiology,* 1977, *14*, 32-39, Figure 2.

refractory period. Data from the P_1 component of the cortical evoked response were of especial interest and were investigated further. Our inquiry was limited to the P_1 component because the statistical analysis revealed that the N_1 latency changes were not reliable and because the

P_2 component frequently did not occur until the voluntary response was over—in other words, P_2 latencies were longer than the RT. We wished to obtain an estimate of the contribution of the latency differences in P_1 that are associated with duration of the inter-stimulus interval to the relationship between RT and inter-stimulus interval. For this purpose, an analysis of covariance was run using latency of P_1 as the covariate. The outcome of this analysis revealed that the latency differences in P_1 associated with duration of inter-stimulus interval could account for about 45 percent of the variance in RT associated with duration of inter-stimulus interval. Latency differences in P_1, therefore, may provide a physiological basis for the delays that occur in the RT when the central nervous system is called upon to process closely-spaced signals.

Cortical Evoked Response Recovery Functions in Children

The material reviewed in the last section suggested that cortical evoked response recovery functions may serve as a physiological basis of the psychological refractory period. If this is indeed true, then we would predict that recovery of the cortical evoked response would take longer in children than in adults. In order to test this interesting prediction, an experiment like the one reported in the last section was performed on a group of children. The results of this experiment are compared with the findings reported in the adult subjects.

Figure 48 shows some samples of average cortical evoked responses that were obtained in a healthy 9 year old child compared with similar waveforms obtained from a healthy 20 year old adult. It will be immediately obvious that the latencies of the major components, namely P_1, N_1, and P_2, of the response to single clicks are substantially longer in the child than in the adult. Figure 49 shows that this difference was also apparent in the group data to single clicks based upon means from 12 children 9-13 years old. An analysis of variance carried out on these data revealed that the latency differences of the P_1, N_1, and P_2 components between children and adults were all statistically significant at the .01 level of confidence.

Although the fact that latencies of the major components of the cortical evoked response to single clicks are prolonged in children is of some interest, the actual delays involved are small. On the average, the difference between children and adults amounts to less than 20 msec, which is sufficient to account for but a small fraction of the difference in

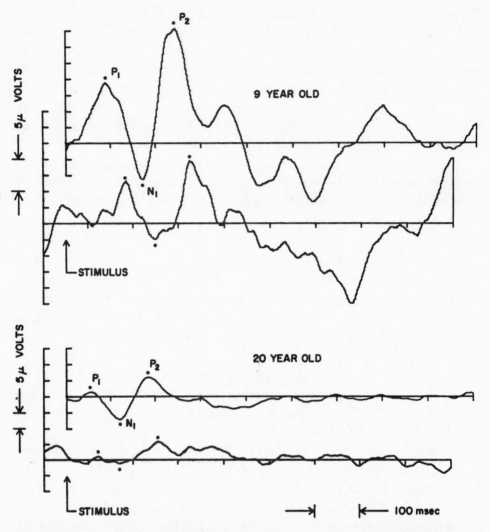

Figure 48: Average cortical evoked responses recorded from the vertex using linked-ears reference in healthy 9 and 20 year-old subjects. In each case the upper tracing is the average response to single clicks, while the lower tracing is the average response to the second of a pair of clicks separated by an interval of 50 msec. Clicks are all 71 dB peak level. Each tracing is based upon an average of 50 responses. Positive is up. Copyright© 1981, John Wiley & Sons, Inc. Reprinted by permission of John Wiley & Sons, Inc. from Surwillo, W.W.: Recovery of the cortical evoked potential from auditory stimulation in children and adults. *Developmental Psychobiology,* 1981, *14*, 1-12, Figure 1.

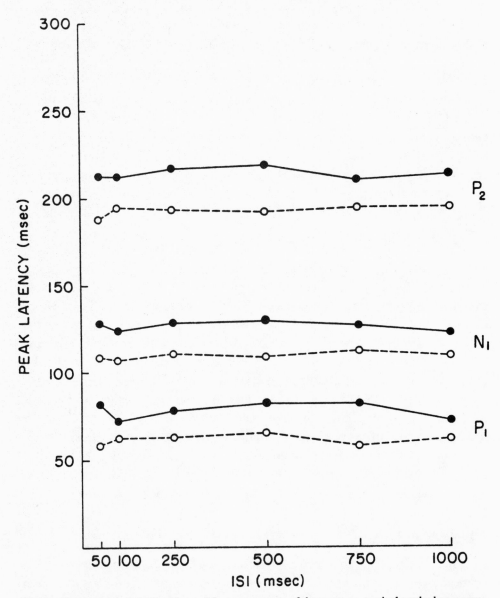

Figure 49: Latency of the P_1, N_1, and P_2 components of the average cortical evoked responses to single clicks in the sequences of paired clicks, all 71 dB peak level. Solid lines are means for a group of 12 children 9-13 years old; dashed lines are means for a group of 12 adults 18-28 years old. Compare with Figure 50. Copyright© 1981, John Wiley & Sons, Inc. Reprinted by permission of John Wiley and Sons, Inc. from Surwillo, W.W.: Recovery of the cortical evoked potential from auditory stimulation in children and adults. *Developmental Psychobiology*, 1981, *14*, 1-12, Figure 3.

the RT observed between adults and 9-13 year old children. Of considerably greater interest in the present context are the average cortical evoked potentials recorded to the pairs of closely-spaced clicks. Through use of the automatic subtraction technique described earlier, these data provide an estimate of the duration of the recovery period. Returning to Figure 48, note that the lower tracing in each case shows the average evoked cortical response to the second click of a pair of clicks separated by an inter-stimulus interval of 50 msec. It is readily apparent from these tracings that latencies of the P_1, N_1, and P_2 components are prolonged in both child and adult, suggesting the existence of a recovery period. But the delays are markedly longer in the 9 year old child than in the young adult.

The group data, which are plotted in Figure 50, show this difference even more clearly, and a statistical analysis confirmed its existence. Thus, analysis of variance revealed that, except for the N_1 component in the adult subjects, the latencies of the three components of the average cortical evoked responses to the second of the two closely-spaced clicks increased significantly with decreases in duration of the inter-stimulus intervals. Moreover, the results of a Newman-Keuls test used to probe the nature of this relationship, showed that the increases in latency with decreased duration of the inter-stimulus interval were larger in the children than in adults. The statistical tests employed the .01 level of confidence, and the difference was particularly marked in the case of the N_1 component. These findings, of course, are compatible with the idea that recovery from stimulation is slower in children than in adults and, hence, that refractory period is prolonged in childhood.

Speculations

The finding that the recovery function of the N_1 component of the cortical evoked response in children showed a marked difference when compared with that in adults raises a variety of interesting questions. Does this finding imply that maturation proceeds more slowly in some brain regions than in others? Would children younger than 9 years show proportionally longer delays in the recovery function of this component? Or would one of the other components enter in? To what extent can the prolonged cortical refractory period observed in children account for a young child's remarkably slow responses?

Until data from younger children become available as well, the ontogenetic aspects of this phenomenon are pure speculation and will remain

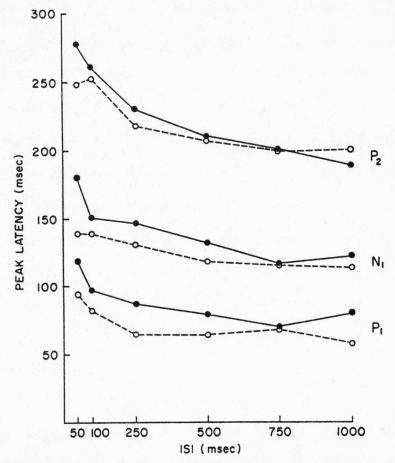

Figure 50: Latency of the P_1, N_1, and P_2 components of the average cortical evoked responses to the second click of a pair of closely-spaced clicks plotted as a function of the duration of the inter-stimulus interval (ISI). All clicks are 71 dB peak level. Solid lines are means from a group of 12 children 9-13 years old; dashed lines are means from a group of 12 adults 18-28 years old. Compare with Figure 49. Copyright© 1981, John Wiley & Sons, Inc. Reprinted by permission of John Wiley and Sons, Inc. from Surwillo, W.W.: Recovery of the cortical evoked potential from auditory stimulation in children and adults. *Developmental Psychobiology,* 1981, *14*, 1-12, Figure 2.

uncertain. Unfortunately, the investigation of recovery functions of cortical evoked responses in awake, alert young children presents some formidable methodological problems. Artifacts associated with restlessness are the biggest problem, and among the artifacts encountered, those resulting from eye activity are the most difficult to control. It is not uncommon when testing children under 9 years of age to find that 70 percent of the data have to be discarded because of artifacts. Hopefully, some cleverly-designed experiments will overcome these limitations so that the necessary data may become available.

CHAPTER 8

A MODEL OF CHOICE REACTION TIME

THUS FAR in our inquiry, we have considered only the very simplest kind of behavior—a task requiring a simple reaction. We have derived a model of simple RT using a few elementary concepts that bear on the way in which the basic elements of the central nervous system function. The basic structure that has emerged from this inquiry is a three-factor model. Simple RT is determined by three parameters: (1) the duration of the cortical gating cycle, (2) the particular phase of the cortical gating cycle in which a stimulus happens to fall, and (3) the rate of recovery of excitability following stimulation of the transmission elements.

The last two chapters reviewed experimental evidence from a variety of sources. This evidence suggested that the three-factor model could explain or account for much of what is known empirically about simple RT and how it varies. Along with the model, a physiological basis for the concepts involved was proposed. Assessment of available evidence relevant to these concepts revealed that the concepts had physiological as well as behavioral credibility.

Disjunctive Reactions

We turn now to a consideration of behavior that is somewhat more complex. The first level of complexity beyond simple responding is a reaction task in which the person responding has to make a decision or some kind of choice before he or she responds. Sometimes referred to as a disjunctive reaction task, this activity can assume different levels of complexity as when a choice is required between two alternatives, three alternatives, four alternatives, and so on. An every-day example of the simplest kind of disjunctive reaction task is when the driver of an automobile comes upon a traffic signal at an intersection that is obscured by bright sunlight so that he or she cannot be sure whether it is red or green. The two different signals are equally probable, but the driver needs to get closer before he or she can decide which it is and make the appropriate response. The two alternative responses, of course, are stop or go; although most careful drivers would include a third alternative response which is to slow down. Everyone who has experienced these events while driving a car knows that, in order to appreciate which light is lit and to decide upon the appropriate response, it takes additional time over and above the time required simply to respond to a changing traffic light. But exactly how much time is involved? And in the execution of what specific kinds of operations is this time consumed?

A Practical Model

The reader will recognize that the simplest kind of disjunctive reaction task is analogous to the case of a simple reaction task when there is noise in the signal environment. A model for this set of conditions was described earlier in Chapter 5 (see Figure 23). The model makes use of a comparator circuit that feeds into an integrator circuit for comparing signals present in the environment with a sample of the actual stimulus held in memory. If a stimulus is detected, the circuit yields a response. On the other hand, if a signal turns out to be noise, no response occurs.

It is obvious that the model we have just now been discussing will also suffice as a model of choice RT under conditions where there are only two alternative signals and two possible responses, one of which is to make no response at all. If the two signals are equally probable of occurrence, then the model will be functioning like the model for simple RT under conditions when noise is as likely to occur as signal. As we have seen in Chapter 5, the operations carried out by the comparator and integrator circuits are clocked in units of the cortical gating cycle. In other words, the minimum amount of time required for a signal to be processed and a decision to be made is the duration of a cortical gating cycle. Because the cortical gating cycle is taken to be the time quantum, any additional processing time needed would require adding the time taken up by one or more whole cortical gating cycles to the operation.

An important modification of this circuit may be made by employing parallel processing of information. Some such modification is necessary whenever the response-no-response dichotomy will not serve the purpose and a unique response is required to each of the alternative stimuli.[1] For example, to use the illustration of a traffic light, suppose both lights are out and that the red light going on requires an effector to elicit one kind of movement whereas the green light going on requires it to elicit another. Figure 51 shows a circuit for doing just that. Note that the circuit is like the one shown in Figure 23 except that there are two comparator-integrator circuits connected in parallel. Signals from the environment are fed into both circuits simultaneously. One branch has the stimulus pattern for recognizing red in memory and, if a red stimulus is detected, the circuit elicites the appropriate response. The other branch has the stimulus pattern for recognizing green in memory, and a response appropriate to green is elicited if a green stimulus is detected.

As was the case with the circuit in Figure 23 the time needed to process a signal and make a decision is equivalent to the duration of a cortical gating cycle, or to some multiple of this value. The latter situation might take place if a signal were run through the comparator a second time to "make sure" that it was a stimulus. In that case, a storage and switching system like the one shown in Figure 43 of Chapter 7 would have to be connected between the receptor (R) and the c_2 neurons of Figure 51.

Disjunctive Reactions Involving Many Choices

Human behavior can involve a multiplicity of different stimuli and a wide variety of different choices even at a very simple level. What happens when our model has to recognize more than two different stimuli and react using a repertoire of more than two different responses? Suppose, for example, that four different signals, α, β, ψ, and ϕ are all possible stimuli and that a different response is required to each? One way of handling this problem would be to add more parallel branches, one additional branch for each additional stimulus and response. But how may we reconcile this with our earlier discussion in Chapter 7 about the single-channel concept of information processing? Suppose that, despite the existence of some parallel circuits, decision making is basically a single-channel operation? Might not the functioning of the model of Figure 51, in which either of the two alternative stimuli can be processed at the same time, be construed as single-channel operation?

---

[1]Alternatively, the strict series-processing model could be retained and a response-selection device added to its output. We have chosen to go with the former; for despite the simplicity of the single channel concept, the existence of parallel processing in some aspects of information processing seems to be generally recognized (Welford, 1980).

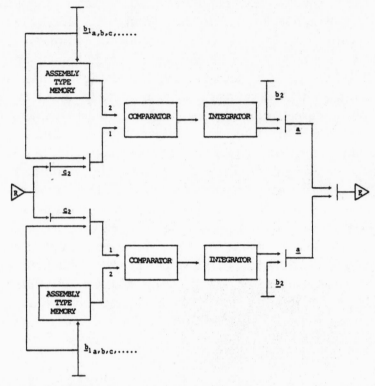

Figure 51: A model of choice RT involving two alternative stimuli requiring different responses and employing parallel processing of information.

In assuming single-channel operation of the model in Figure 51 each of the two comparator-integrator circuits would have to do double duty in order to detect and process four different stimuli. Specifically, a stimulus would have to make two passes through the circuits. During the first pass, a sample of stimulus α is fed from memory into input 2 of one comparator while a sample of stimulus β is fed into input 2 of the other comparator. At the same time, the a neurons would be programmed to elicit responses appropriate to α and β if either of these stimuli are detected. On the second pass, samples of stimulus ψ and stimulus ϕ are fed from memory into input 2 of the first and second comparators, respectively, and the a neurons would be programmed to elicit responses appropriate to ψ and ϕ. The particular order in which these events take place could vary from trial to trial; in other words, the circuits might be set up to detect stimulus β and stimulus ϕ on the first pass. The actual order might even be determined by the system's expectation or guess concerning which stimulus will come next.

The result of making two passes through the circuits in this way is obvious. In order to process a disjunctive response involving four alternatives, twice as many cortical gating cycles will be needed as compared with the number required to process a response involving only two alternatives. Following the same principle, it would seem that six alternative stimuli and the same number of different responses would require three passes through the circuits. But with so many alternatives to contend with, the switching system needed would become quite complex indeed. For the sake of simplicity, therefore, we confine our modeling at the present time to a disjunctive reaction task that involves no more than four alternatives.

Disjunctive Reactions and Information Theory

The amount of information that is processed during performance of a disjunctive reaction task may be expressed in the language of information theory (see Shannon and Weaver, 1949) using the *bit*. The bit is a unit of information equivalent to the result of a choice between two equally-probable alternatives. Thus, one bit of information is processed in the example involving two different stimuli that was discussed in conjunction with the model in Figure 51.

The number of bits processed in disjunctive reaction tasks involving any number of alternatives may be computed from the formula

$$\text{bits} \quad = \quad \log_2 \frac{1}{p}$$

where p is the *a priori* probability of each of the equally probable alternatives involved in the choice. Thus, for example, with four alternatives $p = 0.25$, so that

$$\text{bits} \quad = \quad \log_2 \frac{1}{0.25}$$
$$= \quad \log_2 4$$
$$= \quad 2$$

In other words, 2 bits of information are processed. Note that, in the case of a simple reaction task where no choice is involved, $p = 1$ and $\log_2 1 = 0$. This means that a simple reaction task is a zero-bit task; that there is but one stimulus and one response. However, it does not mean that no information processing takes place during performance of a simple RT task. Obviously, recognizing that a stimulus has occurred has information value for the system.

Predictions from the Model

In what way will the choice RT change with the parameters of the stimulus in a disjunctive reaction task? And how might the choice RT be expected to vary in relation to the various characteristics of our model?

In the first place, we should expect the choice RT to vary systematically in relation to the number of alternatives that need to be considered in the decision. Specifically, the RT is expected to increase linearly with increases in the number of bits of information that are processed. This predicted relationship follows from our discussion of the previous two sections. Thus, for example, if two gating cycles are taken up by a zero-bit task (simple RT) and one gating cycle is needed to process each bit of information, then three gating cycles would be required for a one-bit task and four for a two-bit task. This relationship will be diagrammed shortly.

But now, what happens when the duration of the gating cycle is permitted to vary? For example, suppose we have two individual models; both are identical to each other in every respect except that the gating signals that control the flow of information occur more frequently in one individual than in the other. In other words, the gating cycle is longer in one of the individual models. Other things being equal, it is obvious that the individual with the longer duration gating cycle will have choice RTs that are longer. Less obvious is the fact that, as the number of bits of information processed increases, the RT will increase at a *faster rate* in the individual having the longer duration gating cycles. This is best appreciated by perusing the illustration shown in Figure 52.

In Figure 52 we see how RT varies in relation to the number of bits of information processed, and the role played by gating-cycle duration. At the left, the behavior of two individual models has been diagrammed; the two models are identical except that the duration of their gating cycles is markedly different. In order to relate the models to real life, we have designated one model as being like a young adult subject having an alpha rhythm of the EEG of 12 Hz, while the other is like an aged adult subject having an alpha rhythm of 8 Hz. Also, we have arbitrarily assumed that in the case of the simple RT, or the zero-bit condition, two complete alpha rhythm cycles (cortical gating cycles) are needed to process and execute the response. Following the discussion of the last two sections, exactly one cortical gating cycle is required to process a single bit of information. This means that two, three, and four cortical gating cycles will be used in the performance of the simple reaction task, the

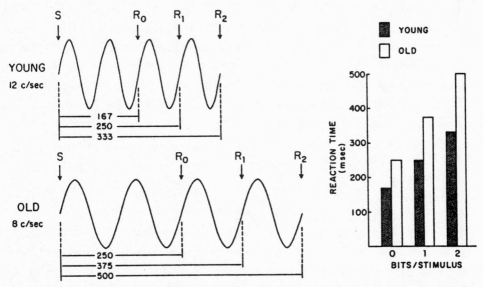

Figure 52: Predictions from the hypothetical model of choice RT. The illustration depicts the responses of two individuals having alpha rhythms of markedly different frequencies and, hence, gating cycles that are noticably different in duration. The individual designated YOUNG, has an alpha rhythm of 12 Hz; the individual designated OLD has an alpha rhythm of 8 Hz. S marks the instant that the stimulus was presented, while the Rs mark the instant of response. R_0 is the response in a simple reaction task where no choice (zero bits) is involved; R_1 and R_2 are the responses in disjunctive reaction tasks in which one and two bits of stimulus information are processed, respectively. Numbers below the waves are the hypothetical RTs in milliseconds; these values are plotted in the graph at the right. Reprinted by permission of the publisher from Surwillo, W.W.: Timing of behavior in senescence and the role of the central nervous system. In Talland, G.A. (Ed.): *Human Aging and Behavior*. New York, Academic, 1968, pp. 1-35, Figure 5.

two-alternative disjunctive task, and the four-alternative disjunctive task, respectively.

Notice in Figure 52 how the difference between the RTs of the two individuals increases as we go from zero bits to two bits and the task becomes more complex. The difference for the zero-bit task amounts to 83 msec. By contrast, the difference for the disjunctive reaction task involving four alternatives (2 bits) is equal to 167 msec which is fully twice as large and is far from being trivial. The histogram at the right in Figure 52 shows the predicted relationship between RT and information processed in bits graphically.

Another interesting prediction follows from our model of choice RT if we consider what happens to the RT in a group of individuals, each of whom has a gating cycle of different duration. In the case of the simple RT, the prediction was already detailed and discussed in Chapter 6. The outcome, as the reader may recall, was a linear relationship in which RT increases with increase in duration of the gating cycle. The same relationship would obtain in the case of the choice RT except that the plot of the latter relationship would display two fundamental differences. Compared with the straight line defining the relation between simple RT and duration of the gating cycle, the line in the case of choice RT would be displaced upward and would have a steeper slope. In other words, the difference between simple and choice RT would be greatest in individuals having the longest duration gating cycles and least in individuals having the shortest duration gating cycles. Or to put it still another way, as duration of the gating cycle increases, so does the disparity between simple and choice RT.

A final prediction from our model concerns what happens to the choice RT when recovery of the information processing elements from previous stimulation is prolonged. We noted in the last chapter that when recovery periods are prolonged sufficiently so they become longer than the duration of the gating cycle, some of the available gating signals are impotent and go by unused. Obviously, the result will be a longer RT. With the recovery period longer than the gating cycle, the time required to process the decision would be doubled. In the same way, the processing time would be tripled if the recovery period were longer than two gating cycles. It should be apparent that in cases where both duration of the gating cycle is very long and recovery from stimulation is slow, the choice RT could become very long indeed.

Figure 53 illustrates the effect of a prolonged recovery period on simple RT and choice RT involving two alternatives. In the examples shown, the duration of the gating cycle takes on two different values, 85 msec and 145 msec; these correspond approximately to gating-signal frequencies of 12 and 7 Hz, respectively. Simple RT is assumed to use up the time occupied by two gating cycles, of which one is devoted to actual processing. The two-alternative disjunctive reaction task is assumed to take one additional gating cycle. The large arrows in Figure 53 designated by the letter "S" denote the point of stimulation, while the smaller arrows mark the times between gating signals actually used in processing. Note that, in the case of the prolonged recovery periods, the arrows are twice as far apart because half of the gating signals are impotent and go by unused.

The histograms at the right in Figure 53 show the RTs as predicted from the models. Note that the effect of a lengthened recovery period is to prolong the RT, which becomes even longer with longer-duration

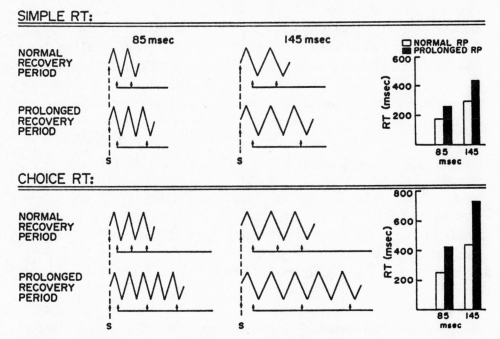

Figure 53: Predictions from the hypothetical models of simple and choice RT in relation to duration of the recovery period (RP) for gating-cycle durations of 85 and 145 msec. Choice RTs are for a two-alternative disjunctive reaction task. The arrows marked "S" designate the point of stimulation, while the unlabeled arrows mark off the durations of the processing epochs.

gating cycles. Thus, for the simple reaction task, the difference between RTs for the normal and prolonged recovery periods is greater when the gating cycle is 145 msec than when it is 85 msec. This difference is larger for the disjunctive than for the simple reaction task because an additional gating cycle is involved in the processing. In other words, the additional information load has the greatest effect on the RT of the individual having the longer-duration gating cycles and longer recovery period.

In the next chapter, we consider some empirical evidence that is available which addresses these predictions. While not extensive, this evidence casts some light on the validity of our model.

Behavior Involving Many Choices — Some Speculations

We can hardly leave the present topic without recognizing some major limitations of our modeling. In our inquiry thus far, we have strictly adhered to the caveat of Chapter 3 against becoming entangled in the topic of complex behavior. It was for this reason that the discussion of disjunctive reactions has been limited to decisions involving no more than two bits of information. Nevertheless, we cannot ignore the fact that much of human behavior consists of simple responses that may require decision making involving a large number of alternatives.

Take typewriting for an example. The standard keyboard consists of 44 different characters; coupled with the shift key, this constitutes 88 different alternatives. It is easy to see that the simple model of Figure 51 can hardly accommodate, by any stretch of the imagination, the behavior of a typist doing 60 words a minute. But if this is all true, of what practical value is the simple model? Can it be of any use in real life? And what can we say about the anatomy of the model that will be required to adequately explain such behavior as typewriting?

While remaining mainly in the realm of speculation, it seems likely that the very-well practiced, over-learned responses that characterize a task like typewriting will require a different kind of model from the one proposed in the present chapter. Typewriting as done by an experienced, professional typist is not simply a disjunctive-reaction task like we have already modelled but having a larger number of alternatives. Rather, it is a complex skill that is usually acquired through long months and sometimes years of practice. In the context of our present theorizing, this practice may result in a switch from mainly serial processing of information as in our Figure 51 model to parallel processing involving many separate branches. In other words, in the case of every-day behavior and simple applications, information may for the most part be processed serially; but in the case of highly-developed skills, parallel processing with a separate, independently-functioning branch for each alternative may be the rule.

The idea that the shift from ordinary behavior to skilled behavior is accompanied by a change from series to parallel processing carries with it certain predictions. Of major interest is a prediction concerning the relation between RT and the number of bits per stimulus in a disjunctive reaction task. We already have said that this relationship should be defined by a straight line such that RT increases with an increase in the number of bits processed. We now predict that, after long-continued practice, any series processing of information taking place originally will be replaced by parallel processing. Accompanying this change, the slope of the line relating RT and number of bits per stimulus will be reduced to zero and the relationship between the variables will vanish. The validity of this prediction will be considered in the upcoming chapter.

CHAPTER 9

TESTING THE MODEL FOR DISJUNCTIVE REACTIONS AND THE PSYCHOPHYSIOLOGY OF CHOICE RT

IN THE LAST CHAPTER, we proposed a model of choice RT that will accommodate the processing of up to two bits of stimulus information. The next step is to find out how well this model fits some of our basic empirical knowledge about disjunctive reactions and choice RT. In addition, we will review some relevant psychophysiological data to see what light they cast on the validity of the model.

RT in Relation to Stimulus Information

The idea that the RT is related to the amount of information carried by a stimulus appears to date back to Merkel's work in the late nineteenth century. Employing a disjunctive reaction task in which from one to ten equally probable alternatives were presented to the experimental subject, Merkel (1885) found that the RT became increasingly longer as the number of alternatives increased. In an often-quoted, classical experiment, Hick (1952a) confirmed the existence of a correlation between RT and uncertainty, and reported that a linear relationship obtained between RT and the number of bits involved in the task. This interesting finding was corroborated in a carefully-done study by Hyman (1953), whose experiment demonstrated that a linear function related RT and stimulus information within the range of zero to three bits. Appearing in the wake of Wiener's (1948) *Cybernetics*, these reports added to the growing body of evidence which suggested that computing machinery and the central nervous system ultimately were destined to share similar operating principles.

141

Other investigations have suggested that the linear relationship between RT and number of bits extends over an even wider range of stimulus information. Thus, for example, Hilgendorf (1966) reported a
linear function all the way out to ten bits. However, there is some question as to whether the task used by Hilgendorf, which involved selecting
a three-digit number by pressing three keys, one after the other in an array of ten keys, qualifies as a ten-bit task from the subject's standpoint.
Rather, this task appears in reality to consist of three separate 3.32 bit
tasks done in consecutive order. Nevertheless, it seems clear that the relationship is indeed linear for up to three bits of information or eight alternatives. As the prediction concerning the relation between RT and
information in the proposed model was limited to an operating range of
only zero through two bits, the model appears to be compatible with the
known empirical evidence.

The Role of Inter-Gate Interval

In the last chapter, we predicted that the nature of the relationship
between RT and stimulus information would vary in our model according to the duration of the inter-gate interval. Specifically, we predicted
that the RT in an individual having a long inter-gate interval would increase with increasing stimulus information *at a faster rate* than the RT in
an individual having a short inter-gate interval. Because frequency of
the posterior-dominant rhythm or alpha rhythm of the EEG is assumed
to be a measure of the interval between gating signals and, further, because aged adults have slower alpha rhythms than young adults, our
prediction compared RTs of a hypothetical young individual having an
alpha rhythm of 12 Hz with RTs of a hypothetical old individual having
an alpha rhythm of 8 Hz. One obvious way of testing the validity of this
prediction is to compare the performances of young and old adults on a
disjunctive reaction task that involves several alternatives.

An investigation reported by Suci, Davidoff, and Surwillo (1960) did
just that. As was the case in Hyman's (1953) study, nonsense syllables
were employed as the stimulus material. The purpose of using nonsense
material was to insure that some of the alternatives were not more familiar to the subjects than others. A different nonsense syllable was as-
signed to each of four pilot lamps that were mounted on a display panel
at the corners of a square matrix. The nonsense syllables were BEP,
BIX, BUJ, and BOZ, and a group of young and an equal group of old
adults learned to identify each lamp by its correct name. After

preliminary training, an experiment was run in which a ready signal was given closely following which all four lights flashed on simultaneously; 2 sec later, one of the lights went off. The particular light going out varied at random from trial to trial, but all of the four were equally represented.

Subjects were required to respond in this task by naming the light that went out as quickly as possible. The vocal response interrupted a chronoscope circuit, and the subject's RT was read from the chronoscope dial. Other, similar experiments were run in which the total number of lamps illuminated at the ready signal was three, two, and one lamps, respectively. In this way, stimulus information levels in the investigation varied between zero and two bits inclusive. The study was carried out on a group of 12 healthy old adults, aged 60-70 years (median = 63yr) and a group of 12 healthy young adults, aged 17-38 years (median = 18.5 yr).

The results of this investigation showed that RT in both groups was an increasing linear function of the amount of stimulus information. This finding, of course, is in agreement with the earlier-mentioned studies by Hick (1952a) and Hyman (1953). Of particular interest in the context of the prediction presently under consideration, however, was the slopes of the lines describing the data obtained from the two different groups of subjects. When these slopes were compared statistically, the slope of the line defining the relationship between RT and stimulus information in the old subjects proved to be significantly steeper than the slope of the line defining this relationship in the young subjects. This difference was significant at the .001 level of confidence. In other words, the difference in RT associated with old age increased as a function of increasing amounts of stimulus information.

Figure 54 shows the results of this experiment for the zero, one, and two bit conditions graphically. Note that the difference between the RTs of the old and young subjects for the zero-bit condition is hardly more than 100 msec. By contrast, the corresponding difference for the two-bit condition amounts to slightly more than 300 msec — a substantial increase. With so much additional time used up in decision-making, it is easy to see why old age frequently has such an adverse effect on the performance of complex tasks.

Similar findings were reported recently by Podlesny and Dustman (1980) in an experiment using visual stimuli. In their study, a simple reaction task and a two-alternative disjunctive reaction task were performed by 13 young (mean = 24.2 yr) and 13 old (mean = 70.0 yr)

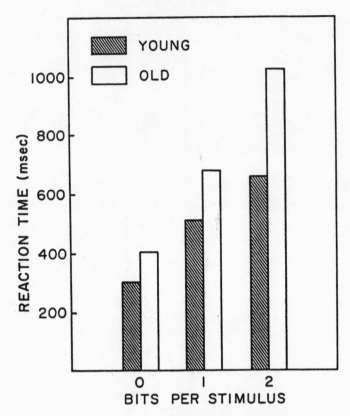

Figure 54: Reaction time as a function of stimulus information in relation to aging in adults. Young subjects are 12 healthy males, median age 18.5 yr; old subjects are 12 healthy males, median age 63.0 yr. Reprinted by permission of the publisher from Surwillo, W.W.: Timing of behavior in senescence and the role of the central nervous system. In Talland, G.A. (Ed.): *Human Aging and Behavior.* New York, Academic, 1968, pp. 1-35, Figure 1.

participants. Findings showed not only that simple RT and choice RT were significantly longer in the old subjects, but also that this age-associated difference was significantly larger in the case of choice RT than simple RT.

A comparison of the data in Figure 54 with the hypothetical data derived from our model of choice RT and shown in Figure 52 of Chapter 8 reveals a striking similarity indeed. The close resemblance of the histograms can hardly be a coincidence. Clearly, our model is not incompatible with the empirical evidence. Moreover, the model is of some practical value in that it provides a simple explanation of why decision-making may take more time in aged than in young adults.

Disjunctive Reactions in Relation to EEG Period

Another aspect of the role played by the inter-gate interval or duration of the gating cycle in the determination of choice RT concerns the nature of the relationship between period of the EEG, choice RT, and age across the adult life span. We noted in Chapter 6 and again earlier in the present chapter that the frequency of the posterior-dominant rhythm of the EEG varies significantly with age over the adult life span. This relationship, in which EEG frequency decreases in old age, may be of substantial magnitude as will be apparent from inspection of Figure 55. Here we see that, while frequency of the posterior-dominant rhythm is about 13 Hz in the tracings from the 35 year old, it is hardly more than 7 Hz in the tracings from the 99 year old. In the light of differences of such

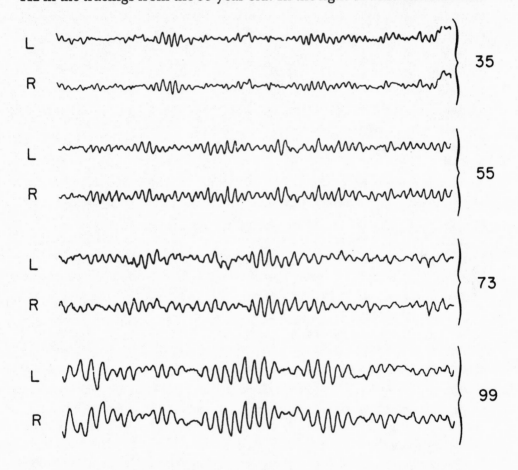

Figure 55: Slowing in the frequency of the posterior-dominant rhythm of the EEG with age in adults. Numbers at the right are ages in years of the subjects, who were all healthy males. The recordings are from occipital regions in the left (L) and right (R) hemispheres, respectively. Subjects were wide awake and alert, but had their eyes closed. The bottom tracing shows a 10 Hz sine wave calibration signal. Reprint of Figure 1 from Surwillo, W.W.: *Electroencephalography and Clinical Neurophysiology*, 1963a, *15*, 105-114, by permission of Elsevier Biomedical Press, Amsterdam.

magnitude, it is clear that the hypothetical gating-signal frequencies proposed for the models diagrammed in Figure 52 of Chapter 8 are not without some basis in fact.

One prediction from our proposed model was that choice RT would become longer with increasing duration of the gating cycle. We expected the relationship to be linear as in the case of simple RT but with a steeper slope. Given that duration of the gating cycle may be defined physiologically by the period of the posterior-dominant rhythm of the EEG, we should expect that (1) for both simple and disjunctive reaction tasks, RT will increase linearly as period of the EEG increases, and that (2) the straight line describing this relationship for choice RT will have a steeper slope than the straight line for simple RT. As the data in Figure 56 attest, these expectations appear to be fulfilled by the evidence.

The data presented in Figure 56 were obtained in an experiment in which 54 healthy adults, aged 34-92 yr participated. Details of the experiment were reported previously (Surwillo, 1964b), but briefly, the subjects performed two different reaction tasks while EEGs were being recorded. A simple reaction task was administered first. In this task, the participants listened for two tones of equal loudness but different frequency that were presented at random and without warning over a loudspeaker. One was a 250 Hz tone while the other was 1,000 Hz; both tones occurred in equal numbers. The participants in the experiment were instructed to respond to either tone, as quickly as possible, by pushing a button with the thumb. The second task, which followed upon completion of the first, required a disjunctive reaction. The stimuli and method of presentation were the same as in the first task; the only difference between the two tasks was that, in the latter, the subjects were instructed to differentiate between the two tones and to respond only when the 1,000 Hz tones occurred.

Period of the EEG was ascertained by measuring the waves recorded in the interval between stimulus and response for the trials on both reaction tasks. For both reaction tasks, average values were computed from these data as well as from the RT data for each of the 54 subjects. These average values are plotted in the graph of Figure 56. In each case, a regression line was fitted to the points using the method of least squares, and Pearson product-moment correlation coefficients were computed.

Confirming what was evident from inspection of Figure 56, the statistical analysis revealed that there indeed was a significant relationship between choice RT and period of the EEG as well as between simple RT and period of the EEG. By apparent coincidence the coefficient of correlation in each case was equal to $+0.76$. A careful examination of

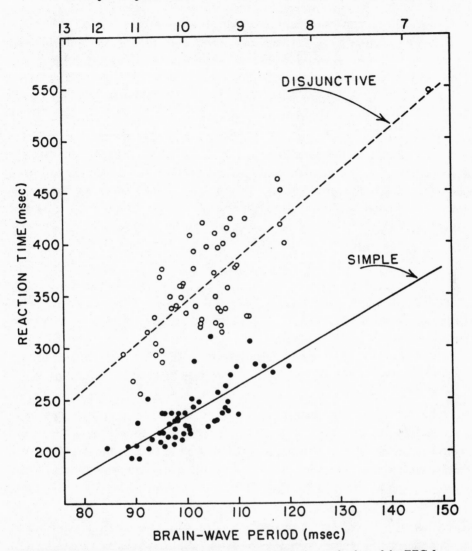

Figure 56: RT as a function of period of the posterior-dominant rhythm of the EEG for a two-alternative disjunctive reaction task (open circles, broken line), and for a simple reaction task (solid circles, solid line). Data are averages from 54 healthy males, aged 34-92 yr. The numbers at the top of the graph refer to the corresponding frequencies of the waves in Hz. Reprint of Figure 1 from Surwillo, W.W.: *Electroencephalography and Clinical Neurophysiology,* 1964b, *16,* 510-514, by permission of Elsevier Biomedical Press, Amsterdam.

Figure 56 suggests that the slope of the line for the disjunctive task is steeper than the slope of the line for the simple task. Actual values of these slopes with their $\pm\sigma$ limits were 4.18 ± 0.48 for the disjunctive task, and 2.80 ± 0.33 for the simple task. The difference between these slopes was evaluated by t-test. The outcome, which was significant at the .01 level of confidence, is in accord with our prediction and constitutes substantive evidence in support of the proposed model of choice RT.

Using the subtraction method originally suggested by Donders (1868), the decision time or time consumed in deciding between the two alternatives in the disjunctive task was estimated, for each subject, by subtracting his average simple RT from his average choice RT. Correlating these estimates of decision time for the 54 subjects with the corresponding measures of period of their EEGs yielded a coefficient of +0.40, which is significant at the .005 level of confidence. In terms of information theory, this means that the time required to process one bit of information—or the information capacity of the central nervous system—is a function of EEG period. This function may be defined by a regression equation in which EEG period is the independent variable and decision time the dependent variable. Based on the data from our 54 cases, the regression equation was

$$DT = 2.33 \text{ EEG P} - 112$$

where EEG P is period of the posterior-dominant rhythm of the EEG in milliseconds, and DT is the time required to decide between two alternatives, also in milliseconds.

Solving this equation for various values of EEG P yields some interesting results. For the group as a whole, average EEG P was equal to 101.6 msec. Substituting this value in the equation, we find that the corresponding value of DT for the group is 125 msec. As one bit of information is processed in this period of time, the average information capacity of the group as a whole becomes equal to $1/0.125 = 8$ bits/sec. When frequency of the posterior-dominant rhythm is 13 Hz—which is the conventional upper limit of the alpha rhythm band—DT by the equation is equal to 67 msec. With one bit of information processed in 67 msec, the information capacity would become $1/0.067 = 15$ bits/sec. It is remarkable that this number of bits is precisely the value estimated by Hick (1952b) to be the upper limit of man's information handling capacity.

In the same way, we may predict information capacity when the posterior-dominant rhythm is at the low end of the alpha rhythm band. Thus, with alpha frequency equal to 8 Hz, EEG P is 125 msec and DT by the equation becomes 179 msec. Under these conditions, information capacity would be equal to $1/0.179 = 5.6$ bits/sec. We find, therefore, that a range of 5.6-15 bits/sec can be processed by gating signal frequencies ranging between 8 and 13 Hz. It will be apparent from these considerations that the conventional alpha rhythm band as used in our model is capable of accounting for a very wide range of information handling capacities.

In Figure 57, the same RT data from our 54 subjects have been plotted against the subject's ages. The solid line is the best-fitting straight line for the values of simple RT, while the dashed line is the same for the values of choice RT. Visual inspection suggests that the slope of the line for the disjunctive reaction task is steeper than the slope of the line for the simple reaction task. This impression was confirmed by statistical test at the .05 level of confidence. These data, therefore, indicate that the time needed to process one bit of information increases progressively with increasing age during the adult years. As period of the EEG and age over the adult age span show a positive correlation, these data also are compatible with our proposed model of choice RT.

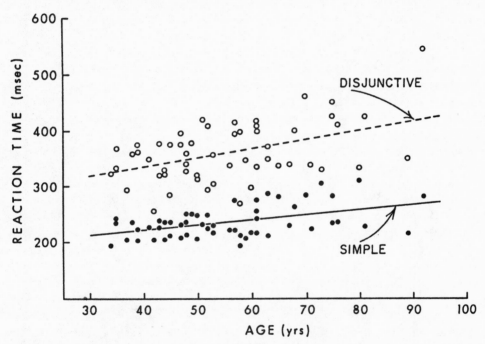

Figure 57: RT as a function of age in adult males, aged 35-92 yr. The solid circles and solid line are for a simple reaction task, while the open circles and dashed line are for a disjunctive reaction task involving two alternatives. Reprinted with permission of publisher from Surwillo, W.W. Choice Reaction Time and Speed of Information Processing in Old Age. PERCEPTUAL AND MOTOR SKILLS, 1973, 36, 321-322, Figure 1.

Effect of Prolonged Recovery Period — Evidence from Children's Data

Data have also been collected in the same kind of experiment done on a group of 110 healthy children, aged 4-17 yr. The findings of this investigation differ in some respects from the adult data and are somewhat more complex as well. To begin with, RT and age in children are not directly related but inversely related. In addition, the mainly linear relationship found in adults between RT and age for a simple and a two-alternative disjunctive reaction task does not hold true in children. This is evident from an inspection of Figure 58 in which RT and age are plotted on logarithmic scales. The fact that the points plotted in log units

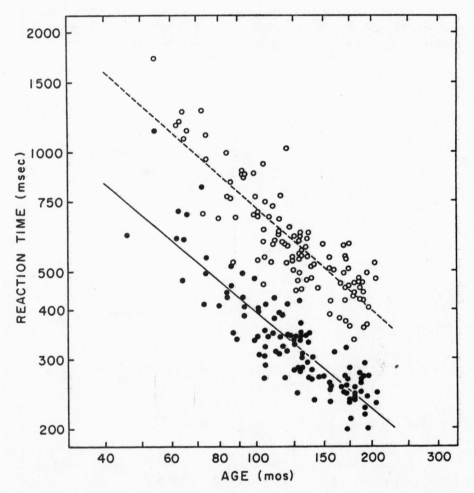

Figure 58: Relationship between RT and age in 109 children aged 4-17 yr. The solid circles (solid line) are simple RTs, while the open circles (dashed line) are choice RTs in a two-alternative disjunctive reaction task. Note the logarithmic units. Copyright© 1971, The Society for Psychophysiological Research. Reprinted with permission of the publisher from Surwillo, W.W.: Human reaction time and period of the EEG in relation to development. *Psychophysiology,* 1971, *8,* 468-482, Figure 1.

seem to fit a straight line rather well suggests that the relationship between RT and age in 4-17 year olds follows a reciprocal power-law function. Equations for the lines after transforming back to linear units are

$$RT_{Simple} = 16,640 \ Age^{-0.814}$$

for the simple reaction task, and

$$RT_{Choice} = 37,240 \ Age^{-0.857}$$

for the disjunctive reaction task.

The existence of the reciprocal power-law function means that RT not only increases as age decreases but increases at a faster rate in young children than in the adolescents. This, of course, differs markedly from what takes place in adult subjects over the life span. Note, also, that the rates of change are markedly different for the two tasks, with choice RT increasing at a much faster rate with decreasing age than simple RT. This may not be obvious from Figure 58 because log values are plotted, but it becomes apparent when we compare the values of simple and choice RT for subjects aged 4 and 17 years as derived from the equations of the lines. For the 4 year old, choice RT is 1350 msec and simple RT is 712 msec; for the 17 year old, the values are 391 msec and 219 msec, respectively. The difference between choice and simple RT at 17 years of age, therefore, is only 172 msec while at 4 years of age it is 638 msec, which is nearly a four-fold increase.

While the last-mentioned findings are not in disharmony with the predictions from our proposed model, they differ substantially from the outcome observed in the adult subjects. From Figure 57 and the regression equations for the straight lines therein, we find that choice RT is 325 msec and simple RT is 216 msec in the 34 year old; in the 92 year old, these values are 420 msec and 270 msec, respectively.[1] Correspondingly, the difference between choice and simple RT at 34 years of age is 109 msec while at 92 years of age it is 150 msec, which is less than one and one-half times as large. Clearly, some profoundly different event or events must be taking place at the developmental end of the life span.

The difference between the data for adults and children is further emphasized by perusing Figure 59 and comparing it with Figure 56, which shows the comparable adult data discussed earlier. In Figure 59, the log values of RT for the simple and disjunctive reaction tasks plotted

---

[1]The regression equations are RT = .938 Age + 184 for simple RT, and RT = 1.638 Age + 269 for choice RT.

in Figure 58 have been plotted against the corresponding values of EEG period ascertained from measurements of waves recorded in the intervals between stimulus and response. The solid and dashed lines shown are best-fitting straight lines; they define statistically significant (.001 level of confidence) correlations of +0.495 and +0.369, respectively, for simple and choice RT. Note in the figure that, despite the fact that logarithms of RT have been plotted, the points display the funnel-shaped function mentioned and discussed earlier in Chapter 6. This

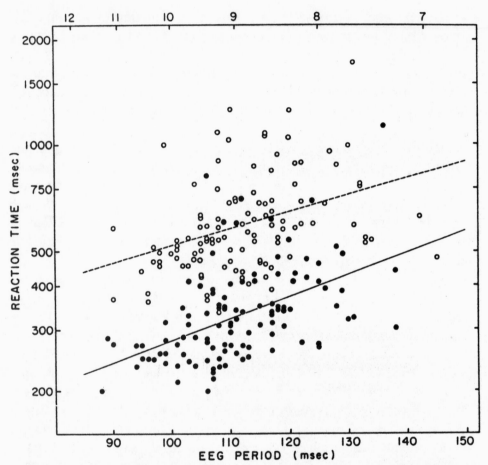

Figure 59: EEG period as determined from waves recorded in the interval between stimulus and response plotted against log RT. Data are averages from children aged 4-17 yr. Solid circles (solid line) are simple RTs, while open circles (dashed line) are choice RTs in a two-alternative disjunctive reaction task. Numbers at the top of the graph refer to corresponding frequencies of the waves in Hz. Copyright© 1971, The Society for Psychophysiological Research. Reprinted with permission of the publisher from Surwillo, W.W.: Human reaction time and period of the EEG in relation to development. *Psychophysiology,* 1971, *8*, 468-482, Figure 4.

contrasts sharply with the points plotted in Figure 56 which are distributed quite closely about the regression lines. The marked difference between the two sets of data seems all the more significant when it is recognized that EEG period covers much the same range in both children and adults.

A perusal of Figure 42, which was taken up earlier in Chapter 7, suggests a possible explanation. As the reader may recall from the previous discussion, there is a rapid decrease in the number of half waves that enter into a child's response in a simple reaction task until about age 140 months; thereafter, the number is substantially unchanged throughout the life span. As we noted at the time, this observation suggested that young children needed a larger number of time quanta than adolescents to process the same amount of information. Furthermore, we hypothesized that this difference might be accounted for, in part, by longer recovery-period durations in the young children which rendered some of the gating signals impotent. The open circles in Figure 42, which are RTs for the two-alternative disjunctive reaction task, suggest that the same phenomenon may be operating in the case of the choice RT as well.

Our plan for testing the validity of this idea was to compare actual data with the hypothetical data derived from our model. The purpose was (1) to find out whether the children's RT data show the same characteristics in relation to EEG period that the hypothetical RT data show in relation to gating-cycle duration when recovery period is prolonged, and (2) to find out whether the children's RT data bear the same relationship to the adult data that the hypothetical RT data for a prolonged recovery period bear to the RT data for a normal recovery period. For this purpose, we used the regression equations defining the straight lines in Figures 56 and 59 to estimate RTs of adults and children who have EEG periods of the same duration. In this way, values of simple and choice RT for children having EEG periods of 85 and 145 msec could be compared directly with the corresponding values of simple and choice RT for adults. The outcome is presented in Figure 60, where separate histograms have been drawn for simple RT and choice RT.

The graphs in Figure 60, of course, illustrate what already has been documented in Figures 56 and 59 and discussed earlier. Simple and choice RT increase as EEG period becomes longer; the increase is larger for choice RT than for simple RT; children show larger increases than adults in both. Of considerably greater interest for present purposes, however, is the marked similarity these data show to the hypothetical

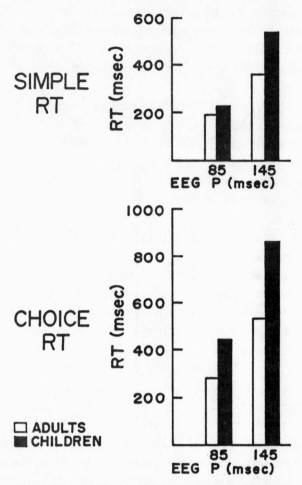

Figure 60: The relationship between RT and EEG period (EEG P) in children and adults for a simple reaction task and a two-alternative disjunctive reaction task. Data were derived from regression equations based upon 109 children aged 4-17 yr, and 54 adults aged 34-92 yr. Regression equations for the children were log RT = .0063 EEG P + 1.8163 for simple RT, and log RT = .0048 EEG P + 2.2347 for choice RT; for the adults, the equations were RT = 2.80 EEG P – 45.38 for simple RT, and RT = 4.18 EEG P – 73.36 for choice RT.

data that were derived from our model and presented in the histograms of Figure 53. Notice how closely the children's data resemble the hypothetical data for a prolonged recovery period; observe, also, how well the adults' data match the hypothetical data when the recovery period is normal. The reader will take note of other obvious points of similarity. What might not be quite so obvious is the fact that simple RT for an EEG period of 145 msec *in children* is virtually the same as choice RT for an EEG period of 145 msec *in adults*. This is completely in agreement with the prediction from the model, namely, that simple RT at a gating-cycle duration of 145 msec in an individual with a prolonged recovery period is the same as choice RT at a gating-cycle duration of 145 msec in an individual with a normal recovery period.

We see, therefore, that all the predictions that were derived from our model of choice RT have been fulfilled.

Information Capacity in Children

Before leaving the children's data, it is interesting to estimate the information-handling capacity of children, and to see how it changes during growth and development. As was the case with the adult data, decision time (DT), or the time taken by each child to process one bit of information, may be estimated by subtracting a subject's average simple RT from his average choice RT. This was done using the data (in linear units) already reported in Figure 58. The result, namely, the values for DT, were plotted against age in Figure 61 using logarithmic units.

The regression line fitted to these points by the method of least squares was defined by the following equation

$$\log DT = -.859 \log Age + 4{,}220,$$

where age is in months and DT is in milliseconds. The Pearson product-moment coefficient of correlation was equal to −0.69; this coefficient was of substantial magnitude as well as being significant at the .001 level of confidence. Solving the equation for values of age equivalent to 4, 10, and 16 yr yielded DTs of 597, 272, and 181 msec, respectively. These values represent the time taken to process one bit of information. Correspondingly, the information-handling capacity of the 4 year old becomes 1.68 bits/sec, of the 10 year old 3.68 bits/sec, and of the 16 year old 5.52 bits/sec. Compare these values with those estimated for adults earlier in this chapter.

Other Evidence

It is well-known that persons with epilepsy show decrements in level of consciousness and impaired cognitive functioning during periods between seizures when the EEG shows evidence of spike and slow-wave paroxysms. Speculating about the possible mechanisms responsible for this phenomenon, Tizard and Margerison (1963) suggested that the sub-clinical spike and slow wave paroxysms reduce the information-handling capacity of the brain. Earlier in Chapter 6, we mentioned a

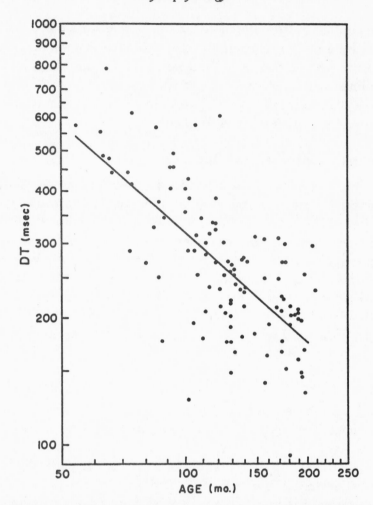

Figure 61: Decision time (DT), or the time taken to process one bit of information in a disjunctive reaction task, plotted against age in children aged 4-17 yr. Note the logarithmic scales. Reprinted from Surwillo, W.W.: *Journal of Psychology, 96,* 97-102, 1977. Reprinted with permission of the Helen Dwight Reid Educational Foundation, 4000 Albemarle St., N.W., Washington, D.C. 20016. Copyright 1977 by The Journal Press.

study by Browne, Penry, Porter, and Dreifuss (1974) in which simple RT was reported to be substantially prolonged during the 3/sec spike-wave paroxysms associated with absencé attacks. The reader may recall that these findings were in accord with our proposed model of simple RT.

But what happens to the performance of a disjunctive reaction task during episodes of spike and slow-wave activity? What would our model of choice RT predict? In the first place, we would expect the slow activity associated with the paroxysmal discharges to result in choice RTs that are prolonged by comparison with the choice RTs obtained when the EEG showed normal background activity. Secondly, we would predict that the choice RT would be prolonged to a greater degree with increasing amounts of stimulus information. In other words, as information load increases, so will the difference between choice RT during normal background activity and during spike and slow-wave paroxysms also increase.

This prediction is readily confirmed by the findings in an interesting study by Hutt, Newton, and Fairweather (1977). In this investigation, 20 persons with epilepsy performed a disjunctive reaction task involving 2, 4, and 8 alternatives while EEGs were recorded. The stimuli, which were presented visually, consisted of numerals projected on a screen. Subjects responded by pressing the appropriate keys in an array; in this way, RTs were obtained for the three stimulus conditions corresponding to 1, 2, and 3 bits of stimulus information. In eleven of the subjects tested, stimuli occurred during periods when the EEG showed (1) normal background activity, (2) generalized spike-wave activity, (3) bilateral spike-wave activity, and (4) localized spike-wave activity.

The results of this investigation are summarized in the graph of Figure 62, where RTs have been plotted against stimulus information in bits for the four EEG conditions. Note that, when the EEG showed normal background activity, RT increased with increasing stimulus information. During generalized spike-wave paroxysms, RT overall was significantly increased (.001 level of confidence); moreover, this increase became larger as information load increased. In other words, the slope of the line for generalized spike-wave activity was steeper than the slope for normal background activity. This finding, which is exactly as predicted by our model, was reliable, being statistically significant at the .003 level of confidence. The apparent differences between bilateral spike-wave, localized spike-wave, and background were not statistically significant.

From these data, Hutt, Newton, and Fairweather (1977) estimated that the information-handling capacity of their subjects during generalized spike-wave paroxysms averaged only 2.09 bits/sec. Based upon our own data reviewed in the last section, this would be equivalent to the information-handling capacity of a 5 year old child.

Another line of evidence derives from investigations of performance on a disjunctive reaction task by patients having closed-head injuries. Interest in the present context derives from the fact that head injury is commonly accompanied by *generalized slowing* of the brain's basic electrical rhythm. In severe head injury, the frequency may be as slow as 4-6

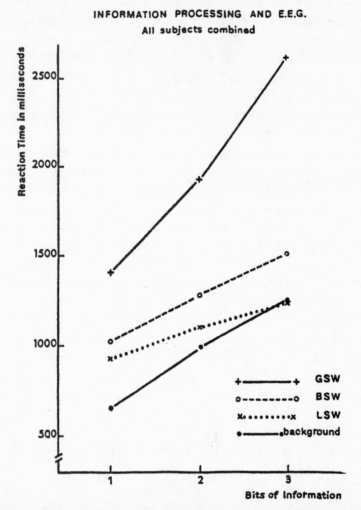

Figure 62: The relationship between RT and stimulus information in bits for a disjunctive reaction task using visual stimuli (numerals). Stimuli occurred when the EEG showed generalized spike-wave (GSW), bilateral spike-wave (BSW), localized spike-wave (LSW), and normal background activity. Data from 11 subjects combined. Reprinted with permission from *Neuropsychologia, 15,* Hutt, S.J., Newton, J., and Fairweather, H., choice reaction time and EEG activity in children with epilepsy. Copyright© 1977, Pergamon Press, Ltd.

Hz, while in less severe injury it may be 7-8 Hz (Kiloh and Osselton, 1966). Such effects have been reported to persist for many months following the trauma. With the basic EEG rhythm slowed in this way, our model of choice RT would predict that performance of head-injury patients on a disjunctive reaction task, as compared with normal controls the same age, would be similar to the performance of old adults as compared with young adults.

Miller (1970) has reported an experiment in which 5 patients with severe closed-head injuries were tested in this way. The patients formed a homogeneous group; all were judged to have a post-traumatic amnesia of over a week's duration but were free of any motor deficit at the time of testing.[2] They ranged in age from 18-28 yr; a control group consisting of 5 persons aged 19-26 yr was also tested. Both groups performed a disjunctive reaction task in which 1, 2, 4, and 8 alternatives were investigated. Visual stimuli were used, the stimulus material consisting of different numerals.

The findings of this study revealed marked differences between the performances of the patients and controls. In both the head-injury patients and controls, RT increased as the number of alternatives increased. The slope of the line defining this relationship was steeper in the head-injury patients than in the controls, suggesting that the difference between patients and controls becomes greater as the information load increases. Analysis of variance confirmed the reliability of this finding, with the groups X conditions interaction being significant at the .001 level of confidence. This, of course, is exactly the outcome predicted from our model.

Parallel Processing—Choice RT and Practice Effects

The design of our model of choice RT is based upon the single-channel concept of information processing. Thus, serial processing dominates its basic functioning despite the fact that some parallel processing is also involved. We noted in Chapter 8, however, that this model would not accommodate behaviors that are characterized by very-well-practiced, over-learned responses. It was suggested that the shift from ordinary, every-day behavior to highly-practiced, skilled behavior is accompanied by a shift from serial information processing to parallel information processing. Accompanying this change, RT would no longer be found to increase with increase in the amount of stimulus information processed.

Mowbray and Rhoades (1959) have reported an extraordinary experiment in which some data bearing on this question were collected. These investigators suggested that with enough practice there may be no

---

[2]The composition of Miller's experimental group contrasts sharply with the heterogeneous groups of "brain damaged patients" used in similar studies (e.g., Blackburn and Benton, 1955; Bruhn and Parsons, 1971).

such thing as choice RT. To address this question, they ran an experiment in which a disjunctive reaction task involving two and four alternatives was performed by a single subject over an extended period of time (5 months) for a total of 45,000 trials! The findings of this experiment showed that, after about 39,000 trials, the RT to the two-bit task (four alternatives) was no different from the RT to the one-bit task (two alternatives). The results, of course are in accord with our expectations. From the standpoint of our model, they suggest that bringing parallel processing branches into existence must be an arduous process indeed. For this reason, it seems likely that series processing will remain a viable concept in modeling simple behavior.

CHAPTER 10

REVIEW, APPRAISAL, AND SOME
SPECULATIONS REGARDING
COMPLEX BEHAVIOR

THE CONCEPTS that we have dealt with in this inquiry have been few; all of them are simple. These concepts have emphasized that time is a major dimension of central nervous system activity. The idea of a central timing mechanism and the role of gating signals in brain information processing were germane to this theorizing. Thence followed the concept of a central nervous system time quantum which found physiological reality in the alpha rhythm of the EEG. Transmission system excitability was expressed in terms of the rate of recovery of nervous elements from stimulation so that time was again involved.

In our basic model of simple behavior, gating signal frequency and duration of the recovery period are the major determinants of the model's—and hence the nervous system's—information-processing capacity. This capacity could be expressed in bits per second, a measure which again involves the dimension of time. Finally, the idea that the reaction time depends upon exactly where in the gating cycle a stimulus may fall further attests to the importance of time.

The primacy of time in the functioning of the central nervous system should come hardly as a surprise to even the casual observer of human behavior. Time is a ubiquitous aspect of all behavior; it is a thread common to all varieties of human activity. Time is a dimension of every mental and behavioral process. The time it takes to perform a task has been used as an index of the task's complexity, the efficiency with which it is performed, and the ultimate capability of the person performing it.

Central Nervous System Relativity

The fact that simple behavior like performing a reaction task shows so much variability both within and between individuals finds ready explanation in the concept of central timing. Thus, time in the realm of the central nervous system is not reckoned by a clock having a beat to beat accuracy of the order of an ordinary timepiece. Instead, variability from one gating cycle to another is the rule, as with an imperfect clock whose pendulum describes a different time interval on each swing. Similarly, different individuals may have different gating signal frequencies in the same way that several timepieces might differ from each other, with some being fast and others being slow with reference to Greenwich mean time. To carry the analogy a step further, children, young adults, and old adults may be viewed as individuals whose clocks are running at different rates.

Of course, the differences referred to become apparent only when we compare an individual's trial to trial performance on a RT task against an accurate timepiece. Or, in the case of different individuals, when their performances are compared with each other and with the timepiece. Viewed in this light, the phenomenon appears as an instance of central nervous system relativity. Nearly fifty years ago, Woodworth (1938), in his historic volume entitled *Experimental Psychology*, predicted that "We may be able in the future to use 'brain waves' as indicators of the beginning and end of mental processes . . . ." The present inquiry, we hope, represents a step in that direction.

But whence might these concepts ultimately lead us? The value of any conceptual framework or model is its ability not only to explain, however imperfectly, existing phenomena but also to generate fresh ideas and new research. In the present instance, we may expect these ideas to be concerned mainly with more complex behavior. It is to this matter that we now turn our attention. For obvious reasons, our inquiry will be largely speculative. Hopefully, however, the speculation will provide some seeds for future growth.

Central Timing in Relation to the Thought Process

While the behavioral sciences can hardly boast of being able to quantify the thought process, it is generally recognized that the thought processes involve the association of ideas in one way or another. Because language and ideas are so closely related, the method of word association has sometimes been employed in the investigation of the thought process. Our present interest in word association concerns the question of how much time it takes. Typically, word-association tasks consist of presenting a single word to an individual with the instruction to respond by saying the first word that comes to mind, as quickly as possible. The latency of this response, or the associative RT, is thought to provide some information about the central processes intervening between the stimulus word and response word.

In the context of the foregoing inquiry, it seems reasonable to expect that the frequency of the gating signals and the duration of the recovery period would affect the associative RT in much the same way that they affect the simple and choice RT. In other words, EEG periods of long duration and recovery periods that are prolonged would be expected to go along with long associative RTs, while short-duration EEG periods and brief recovery periods would go along with short associative RTs. With this in mind, we would predict that word association is slower in children than in adults, and that the associative RT decreases systematically during the course of growth and development.

Associative RT in Children

Although studies of word-association latency date back to the nineteenth century, few investigations have reported on the associative RT in children during growth and development. In his pioneer work, Ziehen (cited by Rusk, 1910) found word association to be slower in children than in adults, and the speed of association to increase markedly year by year during development. Subsequent studies, however, failed to show any consistency of findings. Thus, while investigations by Anderson (1917) and Carter (1938) confirmed Ziehen's original findings, Rusk (1910) and McGehee (1937) found no developmental trends in associative RT. One problem encountered in such studies arises from the fact that the first word coming to mind following presentation of a stimulus word varies from one person to another (Woodworth and Schlosberg, 1954). This complicates the comparison of associative RTs from different subjects in an experimental investigation because different response words evoked by the same stimulus word do not necessarily have the same associative RT.

In order to overcome this problem, the present writer conducted a word-association experiment (Surwillo, 1973b) with children in which commonly-used words were the stimuli and only data of those subjects who gave identical response words were analyzed. Thirty-seven healthy boys aged 8-17 yr were the subjects. The participants listened to a tape recording of eighteen words familiar to children that were taken from the Kent and Rosanoff (1910) list, and responded to each word by uttering the first word that came to mind as quickly as possible. EEGs from homologous left and right occipital derivations were recorded during the entire test session.

Thirteen of the eighteen stimulus words used in the experiment elicited the same response words in twelve or more of the subjects tested. The thirteen stimulus-response word combinations, and the number of subjects who gave the same response to each are shown in Table II. Note that THIRSTY elicited WATER in only 12 of our subjects; at the other extreme, BOY elicited GIRL in 30 subjects. The data in Table II were analyzed in the following manner: For each stimulus-response word

TABLE II

STIMULUS (S) WORDS AND RESPONSE (R) WORDS GIVEN AS
FIRST ASSOCIATIONS IN A WORD-ASSOCIATION TEST
BY N OF 37 SUBJECTS TESTED*

S Word:R Word	N
Table:Chair	21
Boy:Girl	30
Blue:Red	17
King:Queen	28
Bed:Sleep	15
Hot:Cold	27
Dream:Sleep	18
Cold:Hot	19
Thirsty:Water	12
Girl:Boy	25
Chair:Table	19
Black:White	16
Dark:Light	24

*Data from Surwillo, W.W. *Psychophysiology,* 1973b, *10,* 154-165.

combination, the associative RT of each subject was plotted against his age. By plotting both variables in logarithmic units, the points in each case were found to be suitably accommodated by a straight line. Slopes and intercepts of those lines were calculated using the method of least squares, and the resulting data for all thirteen stimulus-response word combinations were averaged. These parameters yielded the equation, namely,

$$\text{log associative RT} = -.4631 \text{ log Age} + 4.1240$$

which describes the relationship between latency of word association and age in children. Figure 63 shows a plot of this equation in linear units. The equations for a disjunctive reaction task and a simple reaction task that were reported and discussed earlier in Chapter 9 have also been plotted on the same axes for comparison.

Figure 63 shows that associative RT is considerably longer than the RT for a one-bit disjunctive reaction task as well as the simple RT. Like simple and disjunctive RT, associative RT varies systematically with age, becoming progressively shorter in the older children. The associative RT does not decrease at the same rate over the years for which data are available, but changes more rapidly in young children than in adolescents. The differences between young children and adolescents are marked. Figure 63 shows that it takes a 17 year old nearly one second longer to come up with a word and utter it as quickly as possible than it does to respond manually to an auditory stimulus as quickly as possible. But it takes even longer for an 8 year old in which case the difference is about 1¼ sec. This, of course, is in line with our prediction.

As was the case in our earlier-mentioned studies, EEG period was determined from waves recorded in the interval between stimulus and response. Values were obtained for each stimulus-response word combination. As it turned out, sufficient data to analyze were available only from five of the thirteen stimulus-response word combinations. Pearson product-moment correlation coefficients were computed between values of associative RT and the measures of EEG period derived from the left and from the right hemisphere EEGs. These correlation coefficients are listed in Table III. Two of the ten coefficients are positive and statistically significant; both of them came from left hemisphere data. Two of the remaining three left-hemisphere coefficients are also positive. The coefficients from the right hemisphere data were all small and statistically not significant.

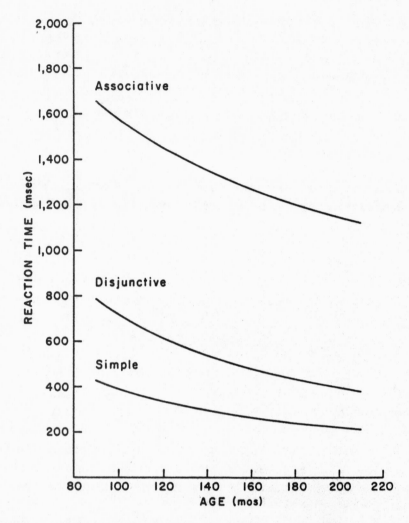

Figure 63: The relationship between age in children and associative RT, one-bit disjunctive RT, and simple RT. The curve for associative RT is based on averaged data from 13 stimulus-response word combinations obtained from an average of 21 subjects. The curves for disjunctive RT and simple RT come from data that were already reported in Figure 58 of Chapter 9. Copyright© 1973, The Society for Psychophysiological Research. Reprinted with permission of the publisher from Surwillo, W.W.: Word-association latency in normal children during development and the relation of brain electrical activity. *Psychophysiology,* 1973, *10*, 154-165, Figure 1.

The data in Table III show evidences of interhemispheric EEG differences, and suggest that left-hemisphere EEGs may have a part in determining word-association latency. This, of course, is largely in accord with the long-standing recognition that the neural structures of the left cerebral hemisphere play a dominant role in the mediation of human

TABLE III

CORRELATION COEFFICIENTS BETWEEN ASSOCIATIVE RT AND
EEG PERIOD RECORDED FROM HOMOLOGOUS LEFT AND RIGHT
OCCIPITAL DERIVATIONS IN CHILDREN*

S Word:R Word	N	Correlation Coefficient	
		Left	Right
Dark:Light	22	.624†	.042
Girl:Boy	23	.067	-.312
Hot:Cold	25	.419†	.219
Boy:Girl	28	-.105	-.037
King:Queen	26	.323	.048

*Data from Surwillo, W.W. *Psychophysiology*, 1973b, *10*, 154-165.

†$p < .05$

language behavior (Geschwind, 1970). The positive correlation coefficients (two of which were statistically significant) are also consistent with
our predictions. However, these findings are based upon highly selected
data and will need to be confirmed in future investigations before any
definitive conclusions can be reached. Nevertheless, the findings provide fuel for speculation. What kind of neural mechanisms are involved
in word association? What actual neuronal events take place in the one-
second interval between the time that a stimulus word is presented and
the response word is elicited? Does associative RT increase with increasing age during senescence? These are questions for future model building and further research.

Control of Gating Signal Frequency

We have noted elsewhere in several places that the frequency of the
posterior-dominant rhythm of the EEG — which we have taken to be the
physiological manifestation of the gating signals — can display considerable variation. This variability shows itself within the same individual as
well as between different individuals. A wide variety of conditions can

affect the EEG in this way. Changes in an individual's state of consciousness, certain drugs, variations in blood gases and electrolyte levels,
changes in metabolic state, aging, normal growth and development,
neurological disorders, trauma can all produce either transient or long-
term changes in EEG frequency. Biofeedback (Woodruff, 1975), Tran-
scendental Meditation (Woolfolk, 1975), Yoga Meditation (Das and
Gastaut, 1957), and even common prayer (Surwillo and Hobson, 1978)
have been reported to significantly change EEG frequency.

A particularly intriguing way in which the frequency of the alpha
rhythm may be changed is by the use of high-intensity, repetitive photic
stimulation. Referred to as "photic driving," this method, which was discussed in some detail in Chapter 6, differs from the other ways of modifying EEG frequency in several respects. First of all, repetitive photic
stimulation appears to change the time of occurrence of individual
waves so that the waves become synchronized to the flashes of light. Secondly, the phenomenon of photic driving appears to be a transient one;
long periods of synchronization are uncommon, and all effects cease after the stimulus is removed. Thirdly, the repetitive or rhythmic nature of
the stimulation appears to be essential for producing the effect.[1]
Fourthly, stimulation by flicker invariably produces some kind of illu-
sory, subjective sensations which in some individuals may be particularly disagreeable or discomforting. In persons who have seizures, the
rhythmically flashing light may even precipitate a frank seizure. Finally,
the nature of the phenomenon suggests that the rhythmically flashing
light may actually be taking over control of the frequency directly, rather
than modifying the force or forces that normally have control over it.
The latter, of course, is purely speculative; but let us see where it might
lead us.

Can stimulation of other sense modalities be expected to produce
similar effects? In other words, can rhythmic stimulation of the other
sense organs take over control of gating-signal frequency? Walter and
Walter (1949) seemed to think so. In discussing the central effects of
rhythmic stimulation of the visual system, they contended that rhythmic
stimulation of any sensory receptor was "likely to produce impulse

---

[1]In an unpublished pilot experiment, the present writer was unable to produce photic driving
of the posterior-dominant rhythm in susceptible subjects when the frequency of the flashes
changed rapidly at random in the range of 8 to 13 flashes/sec. This is in conformity with Walter and Walter's (1949) remark that neural activity due to rhythmic stimulation of a receptor is
capable of reaching parts of the central nervous system that are inaccessible to impulses set up
by non-rhythmic stimuli.

volleys at harmonic frequencies somewhere in the central nervous system." Rhythmic stimulation of the auditory system is common, occurring notably in the course of listening to music. What evidence is there that stimulation of the auditory system in this way can affect the frequency of the alpha rhythm of the EEG and, ultimately, control gating-signal frequency?

Music — Possible Central Nervous System Effects

Although the origins of music lie deep in history, and music as we know it today is some eight centuries old (Henson, 1977), there has been little scientific interest in music from the neurophysiological or psychophysiological standpoint. Yet, knowledge of the profound effects of music on human experience goes back to antiquity. The mood-altering effects of music are well-known. Scarcely a civilization has existed that has not found intrinsic value and enjoyment in listening to a rhythmic patterning of sounds. The idea that music possesses some kind of power over the psyche or is of therapeutic value is a recurrent theme. For example, Robert Burton in the 1630's contended in his *The Anatomy of Melancholy* that music was a remedy for depression and other morbid states of mind. Burton remarked that, "Many men are melancholy by hearing music, but it is a pleasing melancholy that it causeth; and therefore to such as are discontent, in woe, fear, sorrow or dejected, it is a most present remedy: it expels cares, alters their grieved minds, and easeth in an instant."[2] Aside from its widespread appeal, music is accepted even today by some as a useful therapeutic modality.

But what accounts for the almost universal appeal that music has for mankind? Whether it be baroque, classical, romantic, jazz, swing, pop, rock, or just a rhythmic pattern beat out on an improvised drum, people go out of their way to listen to their favorites. If you question them about why they listen, many answer that they don't really know why; some say that they are "turned on" by certain tunes or that some music "sends" them. Others who may have thought more seriously about the question may say that listening to their favorite music can sometimes be a profound spiritual experience for them; but then, they also cannot explain why it is so. Those inclined philosophically might agree with Heinrich Heine, who once wrote that "Music is a strange thing. I would almost

---

[2]Quoted from Democritus Junior (1859), p. 336.

say it is a miracle. For it stands half way between thought and phenomenon, between spirit and matter . . ."[3] In other words, it is virtually impossible to say why we like to listen.

On the other hand, if we inquire more thoroughly into what exactly it is that "sends" or "turns on" the listener, a few ideas emerge that are interesting despite the anecdotal nature of the evidence. A common remark from listeners is that a particular rhythmic passage in the music, or the timing of a sequence of notes, have the most profound effect. This is what most of us mean when we talk about a "catchy theme," a "sprightly tune," a "lilting song," or a "haunting melody"; something in the timing of the notes played appeals to us. Frequently, such passages include the various embellishments that are commonly used in the realm of classical music such as the trill, turn, mordent, appoggiatura, and acciaccatúra. All are a variety of rhythmic decoration added to the basic timing of a particular piece of music. The same is true of the triplet, fifth, and seventh; or, to cite a more complex example, the eleventh or the thirteenth. These singular deviations from the time signature of a piece of music are frequently what make some of the keyboard music of the classical romantic period so rich and appealing. Indeed, our judgement of the performance of a particular work may hinge on the performer's ability to execute these effects correctly.

Recognizing the especial importance of timing in music, we now boldly carry our speculation one step further and propose that music has the peculiar ability to modify the frequency of the central timing mechanism for brief intervals of time. As in the case of rhythmic photic stimulation, we hypothesize that the rhythmic auditory stimulation of music may be able to take over control of gating signal frequency. Furthermore, we hypothesize that the ecstatic experiences reported to take place while listening to music (e.g., see Critchley, 1977a) occur during intervals of time when the gating signal is being "driven."[4]

Unfortunately, little direct empirical evidence bearing on our speculations exists. To the present writer's knowledge, no one has attempted to record EEGs from subjects listening to music for the express purpose of correlating wave-to-wave changes in frequency of the alpha rhythm with the pattern of auditory stimulation. Such a study could present

---

[3]Quoted by Critchley (1977a), p. 217.

[4]It is interesting to note that Walter and Walter (1949) predicted that future research would find a correlation between the features of the evoked response to rhythmic sensory stimulation and "some such character as originality or creative imagination."

some formidable methodological difficulties as it seems unlikely that a point-for-point correspondence would be found between stimulus and response as in the case of photic driving. Obviously, the frequency of the rhythmic pattern of stimulation in music is rarely as rapid as the frequency in photic stimulation. For this reason, the response, if any, observed at the cortex might be some harmonic frequency of the stimulus; in which case, any relationship to the stimulus would be difficult to perceive. However, the existence of the disorder known as musicogenic epilepsy does provide some indirect evidence in this regard. Some evidence that derives from exposure to non-musical sounds is also relevant and will be taken up presently.

Musicogenic Epilepsy

This is a rare but well-documented disorder (Critchley, 1937, 1977b; Poskanzer, Brown, and Miller, 1962; Scott, 1977). Persons suffering from musicogenic epilepsy have their seizures precipitated by auditory stimulation. In some of them, music is the sole known precipitant; often only a specific type of music or even a particular composition is effective. For example, Critchley (1937) reported a case in which only classical music precipitated a seizure, and Tchaikowsky's "Valse des Fleurs" was most effective. In a another patient, Strauss' "Thousand and One Nights Waltz" was capable of eliciting a seizure. Because of this apparent specificity, Scott (1977) argued that the recognition of complex musical patterns by the victim is necessary for the precipitation of the seizure. Critchley (1977b) suggests that the rhythm of the music rather than the melody itself may be the effective element in producing the seizure. These observations, of course, would be in accord with our present speculations.

Although there is a clear-cut relationship between listening to music and seizures in such patients, the possibility that musicogenic epilepsy may be a manifestation of hysteria has been considered. Certainly, the role of music in precipitating hysterical episodes is well-known. The mediaeval epidemics of "dancing mania" and "tarantism," and the practices of some dervish sects are familiar examples of the phenomenon. Nevertheless, Critchley (1977b) and Scott (1977) believe that the well-documented cases of musicogenic epilepsy are unquestionably organic. The fact that the attacks are often accompanied by tongue-biting, urinary incontinence, and extensor plantar responses—and that the EEGs of many affected patients show inter-ictal paroxysmal abnormalities—testify to their organic origin. Scott (1977) has also observed that most cases of musicogenic epilepsy respond well to treatment with conventional anticonvulsant medication, a finding which again argues for an organic basis.

Stimulation by Intermittent, Non-Musical Sounds

Various cases have been reported in which EEG changes and seizures have followed exposure to non-musical sounds such as clicks, especially if they are rhythmical. Only a few of the studies in the literature will be mentioned, as most of them have come up with similar findings.

Gastaut, Roger, Corriol, and Gastaut (1949) appear to have been the first to report on this phenomenon. They used intermittent acoustic stimuli of 8-20 Hz at a pitch of 1000-8000 Hz, and found that this form of stimulation was effective in provoking absencé attacks in patients having absencé seizures. In an interesting study, Kluge and Friedel (1953) recorded the EEGs of 36 normal subjects while they listened to a taped recording of monotonously repeated drumrolls. During this unique stimulation, there was a reduction in the amount of alpha activity in the EEGs. This change was accompanied by the appearance of waves in the theta (4-8 Hz) band. A study by Prechtl (1959) used 139 patients whose routine clinical EEGs showed evidence of abnormal paroxysmal temporal lobe activity. These patients had their EEGs retaken while listening to repetitive click stimulation. The clicks were presented for about 3 min at rates ranging from 1-5 clicks per second. Findings of this experiment showed that the auditory stimulation actually provoked temporal lobe paroxysmal activity in 37 percent of the patients.

None of these studies appears to have found actual evidence of "acoustic driving" of the EEG. Moreover, the EEG changes elicited by auditory stimulation in Kluge and Friedel's (1953) study could have been produced by drowsiness as well. Nevertheless, it seems reasonable to conclude from the evidence that rhythmic auditory stimulation has some kind of activating effect on cortical rhythms.

Predictive Processes

In constructing our models of reaction time, we have followed the plan of a typical stimulus-response paradigm. The basic functioning follows traditional lines. The model is quiescent until a stimulus comes along; thereupon, the stimulus is detected, categorized, and the information contained therein is suitably processed. If a response is called for, the appropriate response is elicited; whereupon the model resumes its quiescent state which consists of waiting for the next stimulus. In short, the stimulus activates the model—sets it into motion as it were—whereas the response de-activates it.

But in serial reaction tasks involving two or more alternatives, this simple plan may not be strictly true. Human beings are curious creatures by nature. Immediately after a stimulus is processed and before the next one occurs, the subject may query, "I wonder what will come next?" Or the subject may say to his or herself, "I'll bet the buzz comes next and not the bell or the gong." Despite the added complexity, this state of affairs must somehow be taken into account in a suitably comprehensive model.

This matter was touched on briefly in Chapter 8 when we took up the topic of disjunctive reactions that involved many choices. The reader may recall that our model of choice RT adopted the concept of single-channel operation. A necessary consequence of single-channel operation was that the comparator-integrator circuits in the model have to do double duty if there are more than two alternative stimuli to deal with. In other words, a stimulus has to make more than one pass through these circuits if it fails to be detected on the first pass through. This, of course, would occur if the comparison samples of stimuli in the branches of the comparator circuits happened not to match the stimulus on the first pass. At the time this matter was discussed in Chapter 8, we noted that the particular pass in which a stimulus was detected could vary from trial to trial in a serial reaction task. Thus, if four different stimuli α, β, ψ, and ϕ were possible, any combination of only two of these stimuli could be detected on the first pass; and the particular combination could change from one trial to the next. We even suggested that the order in which comparison stimuli are placed into the comparator circuits might be determined by the expectation or guess concerning which stimulus will come next.

While a proposal of this kind seemed within the realm of possibility, it was no more than pure speculation. Being far outside the reach of available evidence, nothing further was done with it at the time. Now, however, it seems appropriate to return to this topic as we presently are dealing with speculation.

Forecasting the Character of Future Stimulation

By what means might our model derive an expectation concerning which stimulus will come next in a serial disjunctive reaction task? In the absence of other information, the cardinal rule in forecasting is that future events are predicted from knowledge of the past and present. To use our earlier example, suppose that the stimulus in a reaction task can be either a buzz, a bell, or a gong occurring in equal numbers, and that each of the last two stimuli was a bell. Given this set of conditions, the expectation on the next presentation would be either a buzz or a gong. Or, to use another somewhat different example, suppose again that either a buzz, bell, or gong are possible alternatives but that the buzz and gong each occur quite frequently (say 45% of the time in each case), while the bell occurs only rarely or 10% of the time. If, now, the last stimulus happens to be a bell, the expectation for the next stimulus would be a buzz or a gong. In the context or our model of choice RT, the comparison stimuli on the first pass would be a buzz and a gong. Therefore, we would predict that, in the long run, the RT to either the buzz or the gong following a bell would be shorter than the RT to the gong when it followed a buzz or the RT to the buzz when it followed the gong.

We know of no study in which this prediction has been tested experimentally. One problem with such an experiment is that, without any knowledge concerning the status of the comparator circuits, the findings of the study would not be interpretable. In other words, the prediction of a shorter RT to a buzz or a gong following a bell would hold only if the comparison stimuli present in the comparator circuits on the first pass actually were the buzz and the gong. But how are we to know this? We believe that the investigation of one of the late components of the cortical evoked response in the context of such a study may throw some light on the matter.

The P3 Component of the Cortical Evoked Response

This late, electrically-positive component of the cortical evoked response is sometimes referred to as P300 because it occurs with a latency of about 300 msec following a stimulus. In recent years, this component has received, by far, the most attention of any feature of the cortical evoked response to sensory stimulation. Since first described in a landmark paper by Sutton, Braren, Zubin, and John (1965), literally hundreds of studies of P3 have been reported in the literature. This singular interest derives from the fact that the P3 component is related not to the physical features of a stimulus but to its cognitive aspects. P3 tends to be elicited by rare, low probability events or by stimuli that are meaningful or task relevant.

Most studies in which P3 has been observed and investigated make use of the so-called "oddball paradigm" in which two somewhat different stimuli are presented to a subject serially, one after the other, in quasi-random order; for example, 500 Hz and 1500 Hz tones of equal loudness might be the stimuli. Aside from their being of different pitch, however, the only other difference between the tones is their frequency of occurrence. One tone has a low probability and occurs only rarely, the other has a high probability and occurs frequently; it does not matter which is which. If the 500 Hz tone is rare, a P3 component tends to be observed in the averaged evoked response to the 500 Hz tone but not to the 1500 Hz tone; if, instead, the 1500 Hz tone is rare, the exact opposite is true. Indeed, Duncan-Johnson and Donchin (1977) have shown in an elegant, parametric study that the amplitude of the P3 component decreases as the probability of occurrence of a rare tone increases.

It is this latter finding that is of particular interest to us in the present context. Might not the amplitude of the P3 component recorded during a serial disjunctive reaction task tell something about the expectations concerning the stimulus coming up next? And, if this were the case, could not this information be used to find out what comparison stimuli have been entered into the comparator circuits on the first pass through?

As in the previously-mentioned case, the empirical testing of these interesting notions must await future research. Experiments that have studied the cortical evoked response in relation to the RT have focused mainly on the RT to the same stimulus that evoked the P3 component under investigation. The results of such studies (e.g., Beck, 1979; Ritter, Simson, and Vaughan, 1972; Ritter, Simson, Vaughan, and Friedman, 1979) have been somewhat disappointing. The RT is often found to be shorter than the peak latency of the P3 component—a finding which suggests it is unlikely that P3 plays a role in the events associated with the response. But these studies may be searching for relationships in the wrong place. It may be that the amplitude of the P3 component can accurately reflect expectancy concerning an event that follows; that it sets up the comparator circuits for the next stimulus, and, in so doing, can play a part in determining the speed of response to the stimulus on the upcoming trial. Future research will tell whether or not this is the case.

Concluding Remarks

In reviewing the foregoing inquiry in broad picture, one point stands out clearly above all others. Even though we only considered simple behavior and dealt exclusively with simple concepts and models, it quickly became evident that the probable mechanisms involved may be quite complex indeed. The idea that RT is determined by gating-signal frequency and transmission-system excitability working together is hardly simple when it is recognized that both may vary independently of one another from one moment to the next. The picture is further complicated when we (1) allow the response mechanism to be governed by moment to moment variations in expectancy concerning the features of an upcoming stimulus, and (2) permit the particular phase of the gating cycle in which a stimulus happens to fall to vary from one trial to the next. Without invoking complex factors like attention and motivation, the sources of variability in RT may be numerous indeed.

Our inquiry highlights the fact that the methods employed in studying the algebra of the peripheral nervous system seem hardly equal to the task of investigating the calculus of the brain. But this is perhaps where modern technology may provide some help. Computer simulation and modeling techniques have proven to be remarkably useful in many areas of inquiry. The possibility exists that these techniques may be useful in modeling brain functioning as well. It would be ironic indeed if, after providing the model for modern computing machines, the brain were to have its complexities unraveled by the very device that it helped to create.

BIBLIOGRAPHY

1. Andersen, P., and Andersson, S.A.: *Physiological Basis of the Alpha Rhythm.* New York, Appleton, 1968.
2. Anderson, M.: An investigation into the rate of mental association. *Journal of Educational Psychology, 8:*97, 1917.
3. Andreassi, J.L.: *Psychophysiology: Human Behavior and Physiological Response.* New York, Oxford, 1980.
4. Ax, A.F.: The physiological differentiation between fear and anger in humans. *Psychosomatic Medicine, 15:*433, 1949.
5. Ax, A.F.: Goals and methods of psychophysiology. *Psychophysiology, 1:*8, 1964.
6. Beck, E.C.: Brain dysfunction and evoked potentials. In Begleiter, H., (Ed.): *Evoked Brain Potentials and Behavior.* New York, Plenum, 1979, pp. 269-275.
7. Bergamini, L., and Bergamasco, B.: *Cortical Evoked Potentials in Man.* Springfield, Thomas, 1967.
8. Bertelson, P.: The time course of preparation. *Quarterly Journal of Experimental Psychology, 19:*272, 1967.
9. Bertelson, P., and Tisseyre, F.: The time-course of preparation with regular and irregular fore-periods. *Quarterly Journal of Experimental Psychology, 20:*297, 1968.
10. Bertelson, P., and Tisseyre, F.: The time-course of preparation: Confirmatory results with visual and auditory warning signals. *Acta Psychologica (Amsterdam), 30:*145, 1969.
11. Bishop, G.H.: Cyclic changes in excitability of the optic pathway of the rabbit. *American Journal of Physiology, 103:*213, 1933.
12. Bishop, G.H.: The interpretation of cortical potentials. *Cold Spring Harbor Symposium on Quantitative Biology, 4:*305, 1936.
13. Blackburn, H.L., and Benton, A.L.: Simple and choice reaction time in cerebral disease. *Confina Neurologica, 15:*327, 1955.
14. Boddy, J.: The relationship of reaction time to brain wave period: A reevaluation. *Electroencephalography and Clinical Neurophysiology, 30:*229, 1971.
15. Boring, E.G.: *A History of Experimental Psychology.* New York, Appleton-Century-Crofts, 1950.
16. Bowie, W.: *Determination of Time, Longitude, Latitude, and Azimuth.* Washington, Government Printing Office, 1917, pp. 90-93.
17. Broca, A. and Richet, C.: Period réfractaire dams les centres nerveux. *C.R. Académie de Science, 124:*96, 1897.

18. Browne, T.R., Penry, J.K., Porter, R.J., and Dreifuss, F.E.: Responsiveness before, during, and after spike-wave paroxysms. *Neurology, 29*:659, 1974.
19. Bruhn, P., and Parsons, O.A.: Continuous reaction time in brain damage. *Cortex, 7*:278, 1971.
20. Callaway, E., III.: Factors influencing the relationship between alpha activity and visual reaction time. *Electroencephalography and Clinical Neurophysiology, 14*:674, 1962.
21. Callaway, E., III.: The pharmacology of human information processing. *Psychophysiology, 20*:359, 1983.
22. Callaway, E., III., and Yeager, C.L.: Relationship between reaction time and electroencephalographic alpha phase. *Science, 132*:1765, 1960.
23. Carter, H.D.: A preliminary study of free association: I. Twin similarities and the technique of measurement. *The Journal of Psychology, 6*:201, 1938.
24. Cigánek, L.: Excitability cycle of the visual cortex in man. *Annals of the New York Academy of Sciences, 112*:241, 1964.
25. Creutzfeldt, O.D., Arnold, P.M., Becker, D., Langenstein, S., Tirsch, W., Wilhelm, H., and Wuttke, W.: EEG changes during spontaneous and controlled menstrual cycles and their correlation with psychological performance. *Electroencephalography and Clinical Neurophysiology, 40*:113, 1976.
26. Critchley, M.: Musicogenic epilepsy. *Brain, 60*:13, 1937.
27. Critchley, M.: Ecstatic and synaesthetic experiences during musical perception. In Critchley, M., and Henson, R.A. (Eds.): *Music and the Brain: Studies in the Neurology of Music.* Springfield, Thomas, 1977a, pp. 217-232.
28. Critchley, M.: Musicogenic epilepsy: (1) The beginnings. In Critchley, M., and Henson, R.A. (Eds.): *Music and the Brain: Studies in the Neurology of Music.* Springfield, Thomas, 1977b, pp. 344-353.
29. Das, N.N., and Gastaut, H.: Variations de l'activité électrique du cerveau, du coeur, et des muscles squellettiques au cours de la méditation et de l'extase Yogique. *Electroencephalography and Clinical Neurophysiology,* Suppl. *5-6*:211, 1957.
30. Davis, H., Mast, T., Yoshie, N., and Zerlin, S. The slow response of the human cortex to auditory stimuli: Recovery process. *Electroencephalography and Clinical Neurophysiology, 21*:105, 1966.
31. Davis, R.: Choice reaction times and the theory of intermittency in human performance. *Quarterly Journal of Experimental Psychology, 14*:157, 1962.
32. Dawson, G.D.: A summation technique for the detection of small evoked potentials. *Electroencephalography and Clinical Neurophysiology, 6*:65, 1954.
33. Democritus Junior: *Burton's Anatomy of Melancholy.* Philadelphia, Jas. B. Smith, 1859.
34. Donchin, E.: Surprise! . . . surprise? *Psychophysiology, 18*:493, 1981.
35. Donchin, E., and Lindsley, D.B. (Eds.): *Average Evoked Potentials: Methods, Results, and Evaluations.* Washington, D.C., National Aeronautics and Space Administration, 1969.
36. Donders, F.C.: Die Schnelligkeit Psychischer Processe. *Archiv für* Anatomie and Physiologia, *2*:657, 1868. Translated by W.G. Koster. In Koster, W.G.: Attention and performance II. *Acta Psychologica, 30*:412, 1969.
37. Duffy, E.: *Activation and Behavior.* New York, Wiley, 1962.

38. Duncan-Johnson, C.C., and Donchin, E.: On quantifying surprise: The variation of event-related potentials with subjective probability. *Psychophysiology,* *14*:456, 1977.

39. Eccles, J.C.: *The Neurophysiological Basis of Mind: The Principles of Neurophysiology.* Oxford, Clarendon, 1953.

40. Eccles, J.C.: *The Understanding of the Brain.* New York, McGraw-Hill, 1973.

41. Elul, R.: The genesis of the EEG. *International Review of Neurobiology, 15*:227, 1972.

42. Engel, G.L., and Romano, J.: Delirium, a syndrome of cerebral insufficiency. *Journal of Chronic Diseases, 9*:260, 1959.

43. Eppinger, H., and Hess, L.: Vagotonia: a clinical study in vegetative neurology. In Kraus, W.M., and Jelliffe, S.E. (Ed.): *Nervous and Mental Disease Monograph,* 20th series. New York, Nervous and Mental Disease Publishing Co., 1915.

44. Flavell, J.H.: *The Developmental Psychology of Jean Piaget.* Princeton, Van Nostrand, 1963.

45. Fraisse, P.: La periode refractoire psychologique. *Année Psychologie, 57*:315, 1957.

46. Gastaut, H., Gastaut, Y., Roger, A., Corriol, J., and Naquet, R.: Étude électrographique du cycle d' excitabilité cortical. *Electroencephalography and Clinical Neurophysiology, 3*:401, 1951.

47. Gastaut, H., Roger, J., Corriol, J., and Gastaut, Y.: Epilepsy induced by rhythmic, intermittent, auditory stimulation or epilepsy "psophogenique." *Electroencephalography and Clinical Neurophysiology, 1*:121, 1949.

48. Geschwind, N.: The organization of language and the brain. *Science, 170*:940, 1970.

49. Gooddy, W.: Time and the nervous system. The brain as a clock. *The Lancet, 7031*:1139, 1958.

50. Gottsdanker, R., and Stelmach, G.E.: The persistance of psychological refractoriness. *Journal of Motor Behavior, 3*:301, 1971.

51. Griesel, R.D.: Awareness during abnormal EEG activity accompanying hyperventilation. *Psychologia Africana, 11*:64, 1966.

52. Griffith, J.S.: *Mathematical Neurobiology: An Introduction to the Mathematics of the Nervous System.* London, Academic, 1971.

53. Grossberg, S.: Some psychophysiological and pharmacological correlates of a developmental, cognitive and motivational theory. *Annals of the New York Academy of Sciences, 425*:58, 1984.

54. Harter, M.R.: Effects of carbon dioxide on the alpha frequency and reaction time in humans. *Electroencephalography and Clinical Neurophysiology, 23*:561, 1967.

55. Harter, M.R., and White, C.T.: Periodicity within reaction time distributions and electromyograms. *Quarterly Journal of Experimental Psychology, 20*:157, 1968.

56. Hebb, D.O.: *The Organization of Behavior: A Neuropsychological Theory.* New York, Wiley, 1949.

57. Hebb, D.O.: Drives and the C.N.S. (conceptual nervous system). *Psychological Review, 62*:243, 1955.

58. Henson, R.A.: Neurological aspects of musical experience. In Critchley, M., and Henson, R.A. (Eds.): *Music and the Brain: Studies in the Neurology of Music.* Springfield, Thomas, 1977, pp. 3-21.

59. Hick, W.E.: On the rate of gain of information. *Quarterly Journal of Experimental Psychology,* 4:11, 1952a.

60. Hick, W.E.: Why the human operator? *Transactions of the Society of Instrumentation Technology,* 4:67, 1952b.

61. Hilgendorf, L.: Input information and response time. *Ergonomics, 9:*31, 1966.

62. Hohle, R.H.: Component process latencies in reaction times of children and adults. In Lipsitt, L.P., and Spiker, C.C. (Eds.): *Advances in Child Development and Behavior.* New York, Academic, 1967, vol. III, pp. 225-261.

63. Hughes, J.R., and Cayaffa, J.J.: Is the "psychomotor variant"—"rhythmic mid-temporal discharge" an ictal pattern? *Clinical Electroencephalography,* 4:42, 1973.

64. Hutt, S.J., Newton, J., and Fairweather, H.: Choice reaction time and EEG activity in children with epilepsy. *Neuropsychologia, 15:*257, 1977.

65. Hyman, R.: Stimulus information as a determinant of reaction time. *Journal of Experimental Psychology, 45:*188, 1953.

66. John, E.R., and Schwartz, E.L.: The neurophysiology of information processing and cognition. *Annual Review of Psychology, 29:*1, 1978.

67. Kay, H., and Weiss, A.D.: Relationship between simple and serial reaction times. *Nature (London), 191:*790, 1961.

68. Kent, G.H., and Rosanoff, A.J.: A study of associations in insanity. *American Journal of Insanity, 67:*37-96, 317-390, 1910.

69. Kiloh, L.G., and Osselton, J.W.: *Clinical Electroencephalography.* London, Butterworths, 1966, pp. 79-84.

70. Kluge, E., and Friedel, B.: Über die Einwirkung einförmiger akustischer Reize auf den Funktionszustand des Gehirns. *Zeitschrift für Psychotherapie, 3:*212, 1953.

71. Kristofferson, A.B.: Successiveness discrimination as a two-state, quantal process. *Science, 158:*1337, 1967.

72. Lacey, J.I.: Psychophysiological approaches to the evaluation of psychotherapeutic process and outcome. In Rubenstein, E.A., and Parloff, M.B. (Eds.): *Research in Psychotherapy.* Washington, American Psychological Association, 1959, pp. 160-208.

73. Lacey, J.I.: Somatic response patterning and stress: Some revisions of activation theory. In Appley, M.H., and Trumbull, R. (Eds.): *Psychological Stress: Issues in Research.* New York, Appleton-Century-Crofts, 1967, pp. 14-42.

74. Latour, P.L.: Evidence of internal clocks in the human operator. *Acta Psychologica, 27:*341, 1967.

75. Lindsley, D.B.: Emotion. In Stevens, S.S. (Ed.): *Handbook of Experimental Psychology.* New York, Wiley, 1951, pp. 473-516.

76. Lindsley, D.B.: Psychological phenomena and the electroencephalogram. *Electroencephalography and Clinical Neurophysiology,* 4:443, 1952.

77. Lord, F.M.: Elementary models for measuring change. In Harris, C.W. (Ed.): *Problems in Measuring Change.* Madison, University of Wisconsin Press, 1963, pp. 21-38.

78. Lorente de Nó, R.: Analysis of the activity of the chains of internuncial neurons. *Journal of Neurophysiology, 1*:207, 1938.
79. Lorente de Nó, R.: Transmission of impulses through cranial motor nuclei. *Journal of Neurophysiology, 2*:402, 1939.
80. Lucas, K.: On the refractory period of muscle and nerve. *Journal of Physiology, 39*:231, 1909.
81. Lucas, K.: On the recovery of muscle and nerve after the passage of a propagated disturbance. *Journal of Physiology, 41*:368, 1911.
82. Lucas, K., and Adrian, E.D.: *The Conduction of the Nervous Impulse.* London, Longmans Green, 1917.
83. Luce, R.D., and Green, D.M.: A neural timing theory for response times and the psychophysics of intensity. *Psychological Review, 79*:14, 1972.
84. Lynn, R.: *Attention, Arousal, and the Orientation Reaction.* Oxford, Pergamon, 1966.
85. Malmo, R.B.: Activation: A neuropsychological dimension. *Psychological Review, 66*:367, 1959.
86. McCulloch, W.S., and Pitts, W.: A logical calculus of the ideas immanent in nervous activity. *Bulletin of Mathematical Biophysics, 5*:115, 1943.
87. McFarland, R.A.: The psychological effects of oxygen deprivation (anoxemia) on human behavior. *Archives of Psychology, 22*:1, No. 145, 1932.
88. McFarland, R.A.: Psycho-physiological studies at high altitude in the Andes. IV. Sensory and circulatory responses of the Andean residents at 17,500 feet. *Journal of Comparative Psychology, 23*:191, 1937.
89. McGehee, W.: The free word association of elementary school children. *Journal of Genetic Psychology, 50*:441, 1937.
90. Merkel, J.: Die zeitlichen Verhaltnisse der Willensthatigkeit. *Philosophiche Studien, 2*:73, 1885.
91. Michon, J.A.: The perception of duration. *Netherland Journal of Psychology, 20*:391, 1965. (English translation by Translating Unit, Library, National Institute of Health).
92. Miller, E.: Simple and choice reaction time following severe head injury. *Cortex, 6*:121, 1970.
93. Milner, P.M.: *Physiological Psychology.* New York, Holt, 1970.
94. Mirsky, A.F., and Cardon, P.V.: A comparison of the behavioral and physiological changes accompanying sleep deprivation and chlorpromazine administrations in man. *Electroencephalography and Clinical Neurophysiology, 14*:1, 1962.
95. Mowbary, G.H., and Rhoades, M.V.: On the reduction of choice reaction times with practice. *Quarterly Journal of Experimental Psychology, 11*:16, 1959.
96. Nickerson, R.S.: Response time to the second of two successive signals as a function of absolute and relative duration of intersignal interval. *Perceptual and Motor Skills, 21*:3, 1965.
97. Nunn, C.M.H., and Osselton, J.W.: The influence of the EEG alpha rhythm on the perception of visual stimuli. *Psychophysiology, 11*:294, 1974.
98. Obrist, W.D.: Cerebral ischemia and the senescent electroencephalogram. In Simonson, E., and McGavack, T.H. (Eds.): *Cerebral Ischemia.* Springfield, Thomas, 1964, pp. 71-98.
99. Obrist, W.D., Sokoloff, L., Lassen, N.A., Lane, M.H., Butler, R.N., and

Feinberg, I.: Relation of EEG to cerebral blood flow and metabolism in old age. *Electroencephalography and Clinical Neurophysiology, 15*:610, 1963.

100. Podlesny, J.A., and Dustman, R.E.: Task and age dependency in the relationship between reaction time and P3 latency. Paper presented at the meeting of the Society for Psychophysiological Research, Vancouver, British Columbia, October 1980.

101. Poincaré, H.: *The Foundations of Science.* Translated by G.B. Halsted. New York and Garrison, N.Y., Science Press, 1913.

102. Pöppel, E.: Excitability cycles in central intermittency. *Psychologische Forschung. Zeitschrift für Psychologie, 34*:1, 1970.

103. Poskanzer, D.C., Brown, A.E., and Miller, H.: Musicogenic epilepsy caused only by a discrete frequency band of church bells. *Brain, 85*:77, 1962.

104. Prechtl, H.F.R.: Provocation of electroencephalographic changes in the temporal region by intermittent acoustic stimulation. *Electroencephalography and Clinical Neurophysiology, 11*:511, 1959.

105. Regan, D.: *Evoked Potentials in Psychology, Sensory Physiology and Clinical Medicine.* London, Chapman and Hall, 1972.

106. Ritter, W., Simson, R., and Vaughan, H.G. Jr.: Association cortex potentials and reaction time in auditory discrimination. *Electroencephalography and Clinical Neurophysiology, 33*:547, 1972.

107. Ritter, W., Simson, R., Vaughan, H.G. Jr., and Friedman, D.: A brain event related to the making of a sensory discrimination. *Science, 203*:1358, 1979.

108. Rosenblith, W.A., and Vidale, E.B.: A quantitative view of neuroelectric events in relation to sensory communication. In Koch, S. (Ed.): *Psychology: A Study of Science.* New York, McGraw-Hill, 1962, vol. IV, pp. 334-379.

109. Rossi, G.F., and Zanchetti, A.: The brain stem reticular formation. Anatomy and physiology. *Archives of Italian Biology, 95*:199, 1957.

110. Rusk, R.R.: Experiments on mental association in children. *British Journal of Psychology, 3*:349, 1910.

111. Scher, H., Furedy, J.J., and Heslegrave, R.J.: Individual differences in phasic cardiac reactivity to psychological stress and the law of initial value. *Psychophysiology, 22*:345, 1985.

112. Schwartz, M., and Shagass, C.: Recovery functions of human somatosensory and visual evoked potentials. *Annals of the New York Academy of Sciences, 112*:510, 1964.

113. Scott, D.: Musicogenic epilepsy: (2) The later story. In Critchley, M., and Henson, R.A. (Eds.): *Music and the Brain: Studies in the Neurology of Music.* Springfield, Thomas, 1977, pp. 354-364.

114. Shagass, C.: *Evoked Brain Potentials in Psychiatry.* New York-London, Plenum, 1972.

115. Shagass, C., Straumanis, J.J., and Overton, D.A.: Electrophysiological recordings in the reaction time experiment: Exploratory studies for possible psychiatric research application. *Biological Psychiatry, 5*:271, 1972.

116. Shannon, C.E., and Weaver, W.: *The Mathematical Theory of Communication.* Urbana, University Illinois Press, 1949.

117. Shapiro, D.: Editorial. *Psychophysiology, 5*:299, 1978.

118. Smith, G.A.: Models of choice reaction time. In Welford, A.T. (Ed.): *Reaction Times*, London, Academic, 1980, pp. 173-214.

119. Sokolov, E.N.: Higher nervous functions: The orienting reflex. *Annual Review of Physiology, 25*:545, 1963a.

120. Sokolov, E.N.: *Perception and the Conditioned Reflex*. Oxford, Pergamon, 1963b.

121. Stern, J.A.: Toward a definition of psychophysiology. *Psychophysiology, 1*:90, 1964.

122. Stern, R.M., Ray, W.J., and Davis, C.M.: *Psychophysiological Recording*. New York, Oxford, 1980.

123. Stroud, J.M.: The psychological moment in perception. In von Foerster, H. (Ed.): *Cybernetics: Transactions of the Sixth Conference*. New York, Macy, 1949.

124. Suci, G.J., Davidoff, M.D., and Surwillo, W.W.: Reaction time as function of stimulus information and age. *Journal of Experimental Psychology, 60*:242, 1960.

125. Surwillo, W.W.: The relation of simple response time to brain-wave frequency and the effects of age. *Electroencephalography and Clinical Neurophysiology, 15*:105. 1963a.

126. Surwillo, W.W.: The relation of response-time variability to age and the influence of brain wave frequency. *Electroencephalography and Clinical Neurophysiology, 15*:1029, 1963b.

127. Surwillo, W.W.: Some observations on the relation of response speed to frequency of photic stimulation under conditions of EEG synchronization. *Electroencephalography and Clinical Neurophysiology, 17*:194, 1964a.

128. Surwillo, W.W.: The relation of decision time to brain wave frequency and to age. *Electroencephalography and Clinical Neurophysiology, 16*:510, 1964b.

129. Surwillo, W.W.: The relation of amplitude of alpha rhythm to heart rate. *Psychophysiology, 1*:247, 1965.

130. Surwillo, W.W.: The inverted-U relationship: A reply to Stennett. *Psychophysiology, 3*:321, 1967.

131. Surwillo, W.W.: Timing of behavior in senescence and the role of the central nervous system. In Talland, G.A. (Ed.): *Human Aging and Behavior*. New York, Academic, 1968, pp. 1-35.

132. Surwillo, W.W.: Human reaction time and period of the EEG in relation to development. *Psychophysiology, 8*:468, 1971.

133. Surwillo, W.W.: Choice reaction time and speed of information processing in old age. *Perceptual and Motor Skills, 36*:321, 1973a.

134. Surwillo, W.W.: Word-association latency in normal children during development and the relation of brain electrical activity. *Psychophysiology, 10*:154, 1973b.

135. Surwillo, W.W.: Reaction-time variability, periodicities in reaction-time distributions, and the EEG gating-signal hypothesis. *Biological Psychology, 3*:247, 1975.

136. Surwillo, W.W.: Cortical evoked response recovery functions: Physiological manifestations of the psychological refractory period? *Psychophysiology, 14*:32, 1977a.

137. Surwillo, W.W.: Developmental changes in the speed of information processing. *Journal of Psychology, 96*:97, 1977b.

138. Surwillo, W.W.: Recovery of the cortical evoked potential from auditory stimulation in children and adults. *Developmental Psychobiology, 14*:1, 1981.
139. Surwillo, W.W. and Arenberg, D.L.: On the law of initial value and the measurement of change. *Psychophysiology, 1*:368, 1965.
140. Surwillo, W.W., and Hobson, D.P.: Brain electrical activity during prayer. *Psychological Reports, 43*:135, 1978.
141. Surwillo, W.W., and Titus, T.G.: Reaction time and the psychological refractory period in children and adults. *Developmental Psychobiology, 9*:517, 1976.
142. Sutton, S., Braren, M., Zubin, J., and John, E.R.: Evoked potential correlates of stimulus uncertainty. *Science, 150*:1187, 1965.
143. Telford, C.W.: The refractory phase of voluntary and associative responses. *Journal of Experimental Psychology, 14*:1, 1931.
144. Tizard, B., and Margerison, J.H.: Psychological functions during wave-spike discharge. *British Journal of Social and Clinical Psychology, 3*:6, 1963.
145. Venables, P.H.: Periodicity in reaction time. *British Journal of Psychology, 51*:37, 1960.
146. Volavka, J., Levine, R., Feldstein, S., and Fink, M.: Short-term effects of heroin in man. Is EEG related to behavior? *Archives of General Psychiatry, 30*:677, 1974.
147. Walter, V.J., and Walter, W.G.: The central effects of rhythmic sensory stimulation. *Electroencephalography and Clinical Neurophysiology, 1*:57, 1949.
148. Walter, W.G.: The twenty-fourth Maudsley lecture: The functions of the electrical rhythms in the brain. *Journal of Mental Science, 96*:1, 1950.
149. Walter, W.G.: *The Living Brain*. London, Duckworth, 1953.
150. Waszak, M.: Personal Communication, 1965.
151. Welford, A.T.: The "psychological refractory period" and the timing of high-speed performance — A review and a theory. *British Journal of Psychology, 43*:1, 1952.
152. Welford, A.T.: Psychomotor performance. In Birren, J.E. (Ed.): *Handbook of Aging and the Individual*. Chicago, University Chicago Press, 1959, pp. 562-613.
153. Welford, A.T.: The single-channel hypothesis. In Welford, A.T. (Ed.): *Reaction Times*. London, Academic, 1980, pp. 215-252.
154. Wenger, M.A.: The measurement of individual differences in autonomic balance. *Psychosomatic Medicine, 3*:427, 1941.
155. Wenger, M.A.: Studies of autonomic balance in Army Air Forces personnel. *Comparative Psychology Monographs, 19*:No. 4, 1948.
156. Wenger, M.A.: Studies of autonomic balance: A summary. *Psychophysiology, 2*:173, 1966.
157. Wenger, M.A., Cullen, T.D.: Studies of autonomic balance in children and adults. In Greenfield, N.S., and Sternbach, R.A. (Eds.): *Handbook of Psychophysiology*. New York, Holt, 1972, pp. 535-569.
158. Wenger, M.A., and Ellington M.: The measurement of autonomic balance in children: Method and normative data. *Psychosomatic Medicine, 5*:241, 1943.
159. White, C.T.: Temporal numerosity and the psychological unit of duration. *Psychological Monographs, 77*:No. 575, 1963.
160. Wiener, N.: *Cybernetics*. New York, Wiley, 1948.

161. Wiener, N.: Time and the science of organization (First Part). *Scientia (Milano)*, *93*:199, 1958.
162. Wikler, A.: Pharmacologic dissociation of behavior and EEG "sleep patterns" in dogs: Morphine, N-Allylnormorphine, and atropine. *Proceedings of the Society for Experimental Biology and Medicine, 79*:261, 1952.
163. Wilder, J.: *Stimulus and Response: The Law of Initial Value*. Bristol, Wright, 1967.
164. Woodruff, D.S.: Relationships among EEG alpha frequency, reaction time, and age: A biofeedback study. *Psychophysiology, 12*:673, 1975.
165. Woodworth, R.S.: *Experimental Psychology*. New York, Holt, 1938.
166. Woodworth, R.S., and Schlosberg, H.: *Experimental Psychology*. New York, Holt, 1954.
167. Woolfolk, R.L.: Psychophysiological correlates of meditation. *Archives of General Psychiatry, 32*:1326, 1975.

INDEX